Ghosts of Springfield and Southern Illinois

& Other Haunted Tales from the Prairie State

Rachel Brooks Posadas

Schiffer Publishing Ltd

4880 Lower Valley Road, Atglen, Pennsylvania 19310

Lewis And Clark Monument © Ingrid Perlstrom.
Vector Halloween Illustration of a Scary Night Cemetery © Ecaterina Veclova.
Graduation From Education © Maria Dryfhout.
Piasa Bird © Steve Akley.
Skeleton Hold @ Linda Bucklin.
Photos courtesy of bigstockphotos.com.

Other Schiffer Books by the Author
Chicago Ghosts, 978-0-7643-2742-1, $14.95

Other Schiffer Books on Related Subjects
Chicago Crime Stories: Rich Gone Wrong, 978-0-7643-3114-5, $14.99
Abraham Lincoln: An Illustrated Biography in Postcards, 978-0-7643-2857-2, $24.95
Greetings from Chicago, 0-7643-2545-0, $24.95

Schiffer Books are available at special discounts for bulk purchases for sales promotions or premiums. Special editions, including personalized covers, corporate imprints, and excerpts can be created in large quantities for special needs. For more information contact the publisher:

Published by Schiffer Publishing Ltd.
4880 Lower Valley Road
Atglen, PA 19310
Phone: (610) 593-1777; Fax: (610) 593-2002
E-mail: Info@schifferbooks.com

For the largest selection of fine reference books on this and related subjects, please visit our web site at: **www.schifferbooks.com** We are always looking for people to write books on new and related subjects. If you have an idea for a book please contact us at the above address.

This book may be purchased from the publisher.Include $5.00 for shipping. Please try your bookstore first. You may write for a free catalog.

In Europe, Schiffer books are distributed by
Bushwood Books
6 Marksbury Ave.
Kew Gardens
Surrey TW9 4JF England
Phone: 44 (0) 20 8392 8585; Fax: 44 (0) 20 8392 9876
E-mail: info@bushwoodbooks.co.uk
Website: www.bushwoodbooks.co.uk

Library of Congress Control Number: 2009922712

Designed by Stephanie Daugherty
Type set in Grasshopper/NewBskvll BT/NewsGoth BT/Wingding
ISBN: 978-0-7643-3304-0
Printed in the United States of America

Dedication

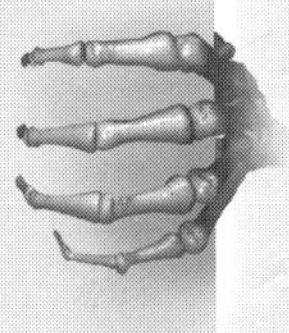

In memory of my grandparents,
John and Rosemarie Brooks:
You are missed very much.

Acknowledgments

There are a handful of people I'd like to thank, including my sister Melissa for accompanying me on the extremely long journey to Springfield, my brother Christopher for the use of his "way better than mine" camera, and my husband especially for always supporting me in everything I do.

I'd also like to thank Dinah Roseberry, Jennifer Marie Savage, and everyone at Schiffer for welcoming me as an author and making every written endeavor truly wonderful.

Contents

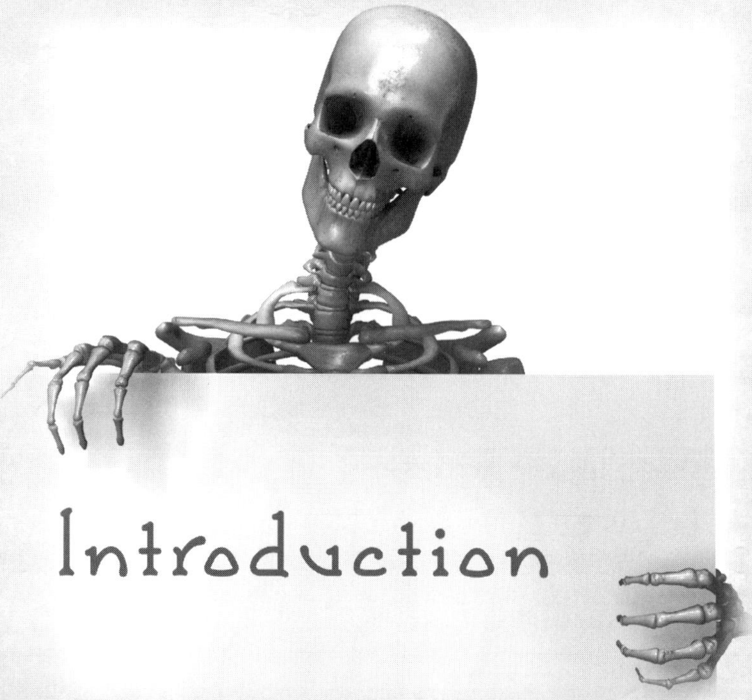

Introduction

Before I began writing books about documented hauntings, I'm not sure I really knew where I stood on the issue of ghosts. I've always had an interest in the paranormal, but I felt more comfortable maintaining a safe distance. It can be scary stuff, after all. When I was a kid, though, I do recall seeing "people" in our house, particularly in the bathroom and my bedroom. I remember feeling so traumatized by what I perceived to be a sinister presence in my room that my parents ultimately relented and switched bedrooms with me. Eventually, we moved into a larger home and everything subsided...but things often have a way of coming back around eventually.

The first place my husband and I ever lived together was a basement apartment in an old two-story brick home that sat directly across from Portage Park in Chicago. Now Chicago itself is known for its many hauntings, but I didn't necessarily think that had anything to do with me. Yet, there was no denying the preponderance of enigmatic occurrences we experienced while living in that house. At first it just seemed like a few random coincidences, but they were unsettling nevertheless. Lights would blink on in the middle of the night, waking us from a dead sleep. Our television, which was brand new then, regularly turned on and off by itself, but it never did that once during the entire two years we lived in our next apartment. There was just something unsettling about that particular place. But of all the strange little things that happened, none would compare to what was to come.

It was mid-morning, probably around ten or eleven, and I was standing in the bathroom brushing my teeth when I felt a chill run down my spine. It was a sunny summer day outside and the house was well lit so there was no mistaking what I saw next. As I stood there at the sink with the door open wide and a clear view of the hall, I saw a man walk right through my house from one end to the other. He moved with such fluidity that he appeared almost to be gliding. His lanky frame was at least as tall as the bathroom door and, other than the distinctly shaped hat he wore atop his head, he had no discernible features. He walked without a sound and looked just like a moving shadow. The most unusual thing about him was that he never glanced my way...as if completely unaware that I was even there. I stood frozen for a moment before mustering the courage to follow behind. I checked the rest of the house, which was only four other rooms, but there was no one. And both the front and back doors were still locked. I didn't know what I had just seen, but it scared me to death.

It would be maybe a year or two later before I finally made sense of the shadowy figure I had seen. I hadn't told many people about the experience. What was there really to say? So other than my husband and a few other people, I kept it to myself. Meanwhile, a friend of mine used to share stories with me about paranormal experiences he'd had or that he'd heard about. In telling his stories, he sometimes used the term "shadow man." Even still, I never made the connection to my own experience until the light bulb finally flickered on. There was a moment when I realized that the term *shadow man* was a befitting description of the strange figure I had seen in my old apartment. I hopped online and researched the term. There was quite a bit of information about shadow men, even drawings of the two most commonly seen shadow figures. To my surprise, one of the images matched the tall dark figure I had seen exactly. I was stunned. Suddenly, some of the experiences I had as a little girl made more sense. Keeping a safe distance from things not easily understood didn't matter and it didn't make them go away.

As you explore the different stories in this book, read them with a light heart and, most of all, enjoy them. The central and southern regions of Illinois are full of historical sites bearing haunted histories. Some of the ghosts you're about to meet are seemingly friendly, while others are menacing. Do your best not to scare yourself too much. Otherwise, before you know it you might notice a sudden chill in the air as the tiny hairs on the back of your neck stand on edge and you realize you're not alone.

What Are Ghosts?

Before we delve into Southern Illinois' supernatural side, it might be fun to take a look at the six different types of haunting activity that can occur, as explained by Paul Dale Roberts, a ghost hunter with Haunted and Paranormal Investigations.

According to Roberts there are six specific types of hauntings: residual, poltergeists, demons, intelligent energy, shadow people, and doppelgangers.

☠ *Residual* hauntings typically stem from extremely traumatic events that end up forging a permanent imprint of the negative experience upon a particular location. For instance, it would be possible for the impression of a violent murder that occurred in someone's home to be re-enacted in that house in later years. Someone could move into the home even thirty or forty years later and begin seeing scenes of the homicide in dreams, visions, or even as spectral images. Many residual haunting activities revolve around negative energies, but it's also possible that strong positive energies can produce residual hauntings as well.

☠ *Poltergeist* activity is often aggressive in nature and involves extensive physical manifestations, such as self-propelled objects flying across a room independently. Many instances of poltergeist activity are associated with harmful and malevolent attacks on humans, sometimes as extreme as sexual assault. Some experts theorize that poltergeist activity is simply a product of an overactive imagination that literally wills the poltergeists into existence. In other words, when a person believes so strongly in a particular notion their mental energy can actually cause the idea to become reality. A great deal of poltergeist activity is associated with young girls in puberty. Roberts suggests that pubescent girls have so much internal energy during this time that it can manifest outwardly via seemingly paranormal occurrences such as flickering lights or moving objects. In some extreme cases, poltergeists may be an expression of sexual molestation.

☠ *Demons*, Roberts posits, are similar to angels in that they never had an earthly physical form. They are purely energy. Their sole intention is to inflict destruction upon the human race. Luckily, cases of demon infestation are rare. According to Roberts, when they do occur there are three possible forms the might take. The first is a beautiful angelic looking one meant to mislead someone into believing it is a thing of beauty so that he or she can be more easily manipulated into doing something bad. In contrast, demons might also present a menacing appearance in order to invoke fear. Roberts suggests this is not a true representation of a demon's actual image, but only meant to frighten individuals. Finally, demons may also appear as a dark hazy image, such as a black mist, fog, or shadow.

☠ In addition to residual hauntings, poltergeists, and demons, some hauntings manifest as *ghosts*. Ghosts demonstrate intelligence and can interact with us. They were once alive and in human form just as we all are. Ghosts stem from the energy that radiates through each of us. What makes the existence of ghosts possible is that energy can never be destroyed. For that matter, it cannot be created either. It just always exists. So even when we die our energy must go somewhere. In some cases that might mean an individual's energy lingers here on earth in the form of a ghost. When this occurs, that person's ghost is often aware of his or her surroundings, including anyone else who might be there, and can sometimes communicate with the living. Ghosts, or *intelligent hauntings*, were once living people.

☠ Another form of haunting activity concerns *shadow people*, previously referred to as shadow men. It is difficult to say exactly what shadow people are. No one has really been able to figure it out. Many clairvoyants and mediums have indicated that they do not believe shadow people to be human. As the name implies, these figures resemble shadows. They are always dark in color and often appear as a tall lanky figure wearing a hat or a hooded figure wearing a robe. Their movements are very smooth as if they were gliding across the floor. They can easily pass through walls and have no clear features about them. They simply appear as dark shadow people. And although they don't necessarily interact with humans, they often produce extreme dread in the people who see them.

☠ The sixth type of haunting activity described by Roberts is the *doppelganger*. Doppelganger sightings are extremely rare and are often associated with imminent danger, even death. The doppelganger appears in another person's likeness. In other words, a doppelganger manifests as someone's identical twin and may even be wearing the same clothing as the individual being haunted by it. When a doppelganger appears to someone it often signifies something profoundly detrimental to the individual seeing it. In some cases, doppelganger sightings are the precursor to a serious life threatening illness or accident that is likely to result in death.

A lot of the haunting activities described by Roberts is pretty frightening, and most folks would hope never to encounter any of them. Thankfully, the most nefarious of them are extremely rare and not likely to happen. If anything, you are more likely to encounter a benign ghost or maybe see a shadow man once in your lifetime, if at all. The important thing is to know that there may be things out there we cannot see or touch, yet it's still possible to see the signs that are already there. Just be sure you're ready to handle the unexpected when you go searching for the unknown.

1

Southern Illinois

Southern Illinois

Southern Illinois has a rich history that reflects much of our nation's heritage. Early activity in Southern Illinois included French settlements along the banks of the Mississippi River, slavery in an otherwise free state, and secret passageways and tunnels of the Underground Railroad. Several Civil War battles were fought on the state's southern soil as well. These things all make for a remarkable history, but one of the most interesting tidbits about this area of the state is its nickname. Over the years Southern Illinois has been dubbed "Little Egypt."

For anyone unfamiliar with Southern Illinois, it might be surprising to discover there are a handful of towns and other attractions bearing Egyptian names. Over the years, different settlements have cropped up with Egyptian names like Goshen, Cairo, Thebes, Dongola, and Karnak. Some have been renamed; others still stand proudly along the Mississippi River as though nestled along the banks of the great Nile. Some folks believe it's the Mississippi River, long like the Nile, that first gave rise to comparisons between Southern Illinois and Egypt. Additionally, the discovery of the mysterious ancient Cahokia mounds near Kaskaskia, which resemble Egyptian pyramids, has also inspired the reference to Egypt. Finally, extended winters and huge snowstorms in past years prompted the migration of many people from the northern portion of the state to the south for corn, grains, and other food supplies. At the time, many people compared the mass migration to the biblical reference in the book of Genesis to the famine that ravaged Canaan and other countries forcing people to travel to Egypt for grain. Hence, Southern Illinois came to be called the new Egypt, and eventually "Little Egypt."

Just as the people of Egypt have struggled at different times throughout history, so have the people of Southern Illinois. Despite being a free state in pre-Civil War days, certain portions of Southern Illinois were involved in slavery. Owners of southern salt mines sometimes leased slaves from Kentucky owners for labor-intensive undertakings they didn't want to do themselves. Slavery eventually came to an end with the Civil War, but then the bloodshed began. The history of Southern Illinois has its share of tragedies, many of which have contributed to its legendary hauntings and ghost stories.

Galena
Freeport
Rockford
Fox Lake
Waukegan
Highland Park
Evanston
Rochelle
De Kalb
Aurora
Chicago
Rock Falls
Geneseo
La Salle
Morris
Joliet
Kankakee
Galesburg
Monmouth
Peoria
El Paso
Wat-seka
Macomb
Bloomington
Danville
Champaign
Quincy
Beardstown
Jacksonville
Springfield
Decatur
Marshall
Effingham
Vandalia
Alton
Lawrenceville
Sandoval
Salem
E. St. Louis
Mt. Carmel
Mt. Vernon
Carmi
Carbon-dale
Marion

The Old Slave House on Hickory Hill

One of the most haunted spots in Little Egypt is an old slave house that stands tall on Hickory Hill along Ford's Ferry Road near the town of Equality. A callous individual named John Crenshaw once owned it. Crenshaw was in the business of selling slaves. Many of the people he captured and imprisoned were freed slaves who he sold right back into slavery. To Crenshaw it didn't seem to matter that the state in which he lived was one where slavery was illegal. He used to hide kidnapped slaves in the cramped attic of his house, chaining them to the floors and walls to prevent their escape. He even secured a "stud" slave, as he was called, by the name of Robert Wilson who later became known as Uncle Bob. His primary purpose was to impregnate as many female slaves as possible, thereby ensuring that Crenshaw would have an endless supply of innocent children to sell into slavery once old enough. It's believed that Uncle Bob may have fathered a few hundred children over the years. Long after the Civil War and the abolition of slavery, Robert "Uncle Bob" Wilson moved to the northwestern Chicago suburb of Elgin, where he lived until his death in 1948 at age 112.

The conditions in which Crenshaw illegally confined enslaved victims within his attic were inhumane: ventilation was poor, there was very little light, and there was no room to move around. Crenshaw even had a hidden tunnel through which slaves were secretly transported from a boat on the river to his home without anyone in the community ever knowing what he was up to. Crenshaw ran a successful farm and salt mining business and could easily launder any funds made through illegal slave trafficking into his legitimate business. In order to ensure the success of his slave trade, Crenshaw hired a group of men called Night Riders to search for and capture escaped slaves. Both Crenshaw's salt business and his illegal slave trade prospered for several years, until he was indicted in 1842 for kidnapping a free black woman and her children. After this, his farming and salt business began to suffer as well. Some folks even retaliated by burning down one of his mills. And if that wasn't enough difficulty for Crenshaw, a slave chopped one of his legs off with an ax in defense of another slave who was being severely beaten at the time. Crenshaw ended up moving and branched out from farming to lumber, railroads, and banking until he passed away in 1871 and was buried near his old slave house in the Hickory Hill Cemetery.

After Crenshaw sold the old slave house and moved a little further away, the new owners left the remnants of the attic slave quarters intact. Rumor has it that Crenshaw continued hiding slaves in the house to be sold later and paid the new owner off to keep quiet. Whether or not that is true is unknown, but it can be said with absolute certainty that Crenshaw operated an illegal slave trade from the house during the time he still owned it. Even today, the house bears signs of the atrocities that once occurred there. Depressions are still visible in the wood walls and floor of the attic where heavy chains were used to restrain slaves. The history of the place is also evident in the balls and chains still on display there. But those aren't the only remnants of the house's terrible history. Some say the spirits of the slaves once hidden away there now haunt the attic.

Over the years numerous visitors have made their way to historic Hickory Hill, curious about the old slave house. Most folks have only expected to simply see the grounds, its secret tunnels, and the tiny attic divided into individual cells with balls and chains for shackling kidnapped slaves. What they didn't bargain for were the supernatural sounds of pained cries and moans, as well as the heavy dragging of metal chains across the worn wood floor. Others have heard the soft, low singing of spiritual hymns coming from the attic. Still, other experiences include random cold spots, overwhelming feelings of sorrow and fear, and the gentle brush of invisible hands. The old slave house was open to visitors for years and it was possible to experience the hauntings first hand. Unfortunately, the house had to be closed to the public in 1996 due to a lack of funding. So for the present, visitors are no longer permitted inside, but the house *isn't* empty—it's still filled with the trapped souls of the slaves who had were imprisoned there in life.

Salem's McMackin House

If you ever happen to drive through historic downtown Salem, you won't want to miss passing by the McMackin House on North Broadway. Long purported to be haunted by members of the McMackin family, the beloved house that proudly served as their home for decades was eventually transformed into a restaurant. New owners purchased the property in 1995 following the death of Flora McMackin, the last of the McMackin family members to have lived in the house. With the home's great location, the new owners thought it would be the perfect place for a restaurant, but things weren't so perfect. The struggling restaurant passed hands many times, and was seemingly cursed as each restaurant venture failed. Some people believe members of the McMackin family may have had something to do with the restaurant's demise.

There was a short period of time when the restaurant business thrived there, and it might have had quite a lot to do with the presence of some McMackin spirits. When new owners again took over the restaurant in 2002, they were given several portraits of various McMackin family members by surviving relatives. When the pictures were set aside rather than immediately put up on the walls, strange things started happening. Existing pictures that were already hanging were knocked to the ground by a seemingly angry force. Various items were often pushed off the fireplace mantel, and other random items were broken. Once the McMackin family portraits were finally placed square and center on the walls of the restaurant, all the hostile paranormal activity died down...but that doesn't mean *it* ended altogether. Other hauntings in the restaurant have included items being mysteriously relocated, uncharacteristic cold spots, and ghostly figures lurking in the shadows. McMackin relatives still living in the area believe the family member responsible for most of the activity is Aunt Helen, who always had a strong affinity for the house and liked playing jokes on people. An uncle is also believed to haunt the building. His deep jovial laughter can sometimes be heard accompanied by the sweet aroma of his tobacco pipe. Another spirit, that may or may not be Aunt Helen, was known to haunt the ladies restroom when the restaurant was still in operation. Now there is no longer a restaurant in the building, but the paranormal activity seems to persist.

So what's with the McMackin family? Why are they haunting the old house? Did they simply love it so much that they've held on to it even in death? The McMackins were a well-known family around Salem. In fact, five different McMackin men served as mayor at various times in Salem's history. Mayor Warren McMackin's son Charles built the home that is now known as the McMackin House. Charles McMackin lived there with his wife Eugenia and their two children, Omar and Helen. Much of the eventual paranormal activity in the house would stem from these two. As you might have guessed, young Helen and the infamous spirit of Aunt Helen, who now seems to haunt the house, are one in the same. Aunt Helen never married, instead living in the family home throughout her adult life and devoting much of her time to the family business — a funeral home — that operated out of the house. Now what about Helen's brother Omar? Omar McMackin married a woman named Mary Belle Wells. They had two children, Matthew and Charles, but Matthew died from the flu when he was still just an infant. Within six months of his death, his mother Mary Belle would also pass after her hair caught fire on the stove and she burned to death. Her surviving son, Charles, was only three years old when it happened and was left in the care of his Aunt Helen while his father went off to fight in World War I. Following these horrific family tragedies, several unexplained happenings began to occur. Baby Matthew soft cries are often heard in the house. His mother's spirit, meanwhile, was previously in the habit of requesting a table for one during the restaurant's run before ultimately vanishing into thin air. And don't forget about the spirit of Aunt Helen who likes to play pranks on unsuspecting folks. It's not certain who the man with the pipe is, but it could very well be Helen's brother and Mary Belle's husband, Omar McMackin. Overall, these ghosts seem to be fun-loving and don't necessarily mean any harm. So if you ever find yourself the victim of one of Aunt Helen's pranks, don't take it too personally. She does that to everyone.

Elizabethtown's Grand Rose Hotel

The Grand Rose Hotel in Elizabethtown was built by the McFarlan family (later changed to McFarland) in 1812 high up on the limestone bluffs overlooking the Ohio River. The building originally only housed a tavern, but soon transformed into the McFarlan Hotel after additional rooms were constructed that could be rented out to the many visitors traveling along the river. The hotel's present day name was chosen for a later owner, Sarah Rose, who purchased the place in 1891 after having been employed there for seven years. Upon acquiring the hotel, she promptly renamed it the Rose Hotel. It certainly was grand in its day, just as its name now implies. Unfortunately, though, the years were not kind to the Grand Rose and it eventually struggled as business waned, especially after Sarah's death in 1939. In 1989 the State of Illinois Historic Preservation Society bought the property, closed the hotel, and began much needed renovations. In time the hotel opened again and began operating as a bed and breakfast as it still does today. The newly revamped bed and breakfast is quite charming and the view overlooking the Ohio River is breathtaking, but there is one strange feature to the place. The backyard area of the hotel still sports a small family graveyard where members of the McFarlan family are buried. Imagine sleeping just a few yards away from a graveyard! Stranger still are the ghosts of former guests who've never checked out. So far they seem harmless, but it's a little unsettling to have your room door open without warning by an invisible energy or to hear ghostly footsteps tapping along the hallway floor as they pass by your room. If you ever do take a respite at the Grand Rose Hotel Bed & Breakfast, there probably isn't much reason to worry about the ghosts, but you should be sure to ask about the massive floods of 1913 and 1937 when river waters rose all the way up over the high limestone bluffs covering the grounds of the hotel.

Jonesboro's Dug Hill Lane

There's a bizarre story that's been passed around Jonesboro for several generations of a supernatural creature that is more of a boogey man than a ghost. This boogey man, initially called either the "boger" or "booger," was first spotted along a dirt road running through Jonesboro called Dug Hill Lane. The isolated stretch of road was once a treacherous route that often put lonely travelers at risk of being robbed or assaulted. One frightening encounter pitted a worried husband against a formidable opponent. Frank Corzine was traveling along Dug Hill Lane in the middle of the night to retrieve the local doctor for his ailing wife. On most trips down the desolate road it was uncommon to pass another traveler, but on that particular night there was someone else on the road. An ominous looking man who stood at least ten feet tall suddenly appeared in the road out of nowhere. Corzine was startled at first, but not immediately alarmed. That was until the huge man began chasing after him. He seemed to run faster than was humanly possible and almost managed to catch up with Corzine. When Corzine finally arrived at the doctor's house, he was terrified beyond measure. Once he began to regain his composure he relayed the story of the strange man he had encountered along Dug Hill Lane. Surprisingly, the doctor had seen the same creature several nights earlier wearing the same black pants, white shirt, and long scarf Corzine had seen him in. Was this superhuman man simply an oversized vagabond attempting to mug unsuspecting travelers or was it something more sinister like the boogey man?

In addition to the baffling sightings of the alleged boogey man, a few apparitions have been spotted along Dug Hill Lane as well. At times a phantom prairie wagon drawn by two tall jet black horses has been seen traveling down the dusty road even though the days of covered wagons are long behind us. The other spectral sighting along Dug Hill Lane is that of a former Civil War military commander named Welch who was ruthlessly killed in 1865 by his own men. The unexpected ambush that robbed him of his life seems to have compelled him to wander the barren roadway near where he was so callously snuffed out by the men he trusted most. Now his ghost occasionally wanders aimlessly along Dug Hill Lane, perhaps searching for some new friends.

Carbondale

For many folks, the town of Carbondale is most closely associated with Southern Illinois University. For others, it's also the location of one of the most haunted houses in the entire Little Egypt area, the Hundley House. The home was built in 1915 and was occupied by former Carbondale mayor Charles Hundley. Mr. Hundley and his wife Luella lived there alone, however, Victor, Mrs. Hundley's son from a previous marriage, happened to live next door. The Hundleys lived a happy life that was, unfortunately, cut short. One chilly night in December, as Mr. Hundley was getting ready for bed in an upstairs bedroom and Mrs. Hundley was tidying up downstairs, the couple was startled by an intruder. Strangely enough, the trespasser was already on the upper floor waiting for someone to come up. Mr. Hundley was the first one upstairs and as he sat down on the edge of the bed he was shot in the back of the head with a .45 caliber revolver. Mrs. Hundley heard the loud bang and ran from the kitchen toward the back staircase leading up to the bedroom where her husband had just been shot. As the intruder made his way down the staircase he came upon Mrs. Hundley and shot her three times, twice in the head and once directly in the heart. She collapsed at the bottom of the staircase and the offender quietly made his way through the kitchen and out the back door.

When police and investigators arrived at the bloody crime scene a little later, they were surprised to find that all the lights in the house had been turned off as if the Hundleys had already retired to bed for the night, yet that wasn't the case. That seemingly small fact would soon lead them to suspect the killer was someone familiar with the layout of the house, like a family member for instance, and that he or she had turned all the lights off on their way out. The killer may have hoped no one would notice anything until the following morning and just assume the Hundleys were sound asleep for the night. Another fact that suggested the killer was someone close to the family was that nothing was missing, so robbery was ruled out as a motive. The killings were either completely random or deeply personal. As investigators gathered evidence, the clues soon pointed in the direction of Mr. Hundley's stepson Victor, who had a professional falling out with Mr. Hundley. Sadly, investigators were never able to successfully solve the case. If Victor was the killer, he walked free and no one else was ever charged with the crimes.

The cruel fate suffered by the Hundleys may have cut their lives short, but it hasn't stopped them from continuing to enjoy their home together. After the house was sold, it didn't take long for the new owners to notice several unexplained occurrences. Voices could often be heard near the back staircase where Mrs. Hundley was shot. Lights in the house regularly turn on and off on their own, doors open and close, and the porch swing sometimes rocks back and forth even when there's no breeze to push it. Other strange sightings have included the sound of gunshots and a quick flash of light in the upstairs bedroom as though the gruesome scene were replaying itself over and over. In time the house was converted to chiropractic offices as the home's tragic past was simply too overwhelming for anyone to live there anymore.

☠☠☠☠☠

Prairie Du Rocher

The small town of Prairie du Rocher is located just fifteen miles south of East St. Louis on the Illinois side of the river and was established by French settlers. There are two major hauntings here. The first centers on a home known as the Creole House and the second is a phantom funeral that travels from an old military post called Old Fort de Chartres.

The Creole House was built in the 1800s—the exact date unknown—and was later purchased by the Brickey family in 1855. It's the spirits of the Brickey family that are believed to now haunt the house, which is highly probable considering the Brickey family cemetery sits right outside in the backyard of this historic landmark. Within the confines of the cemetery, electrical equipment generally stops working and does not return to normal until safely outside the cemetery again. Inside the house, ghostly voices have been heard, as have phantom footsteps creaking across the floorboards of the dusty attic. Cold spots have been felt at times and a shadowy skull image has been seen on the wall many times. Lights turn on and off by themselves and it's not uncommon for doors to loudly slam shut during the night. The presence of paranormal activity is also denoted by the scent of a woman's perfume wafting through the house on occasion.

Old Fort de Chartres was an early French military post that was used as early as the 1700s. All that remains today of the former fortress is its foundation and a handful of the original buildings that were salvaged and restored at one time. Over the years this former military fort has come to be associated with a bizarre phantom funeral procession that only appears to three individuals around midnight on the Fourth of July in years when the date falls on a Friday. The first sighting was in 1889 and the most recent occurrence was in 2008, so if you've never seen it you'll have to wait until 2014 when July 4th once again falls on a Friday. If you're around for it when it happens again, what you'll see is a large wagon-covered funeral procession transporting a casket from the old fort down a dusty road toward a nearby cemetery. Despite the sizeable group, not a sound will be heard. You won't hear the wagon wheels spinning nor will you hear the clomping of horse hoofs. The entire procession will pass by in complete silence as if it was a scene from a silent movie from yesteryear.

So who is the phantom funeral for? Some accounts indicate that a local Prairie du Rocher man got into an argument with one of the military officers stationed at the fort while it was still in operation. Angry tempers and harsh words quickly turned into a full-fledged brawl that ended in the local man's death. In order to keep the incident under wraps, military officers planned to bury the man at a nearby cemetery under the cloak of night when no one would see. A full military funeral procession was ordered so that in the event anyone did observe the ceremony they would simply conclude it was for a military officer killed in battle. Other accounts suggest it was actually two officers who fought to the death for the affections of a young woman. Either way, you can see for yourself when the phantom funeral procession next travels at midnight on July 4, 2014.

☠☠☠☠☠

Okawville

In the small town of Okawville, on North Hanover Street, sits an extremely haunted hotel named the Original Mineral Springs Hotel. Before a hotel stood on the site the original owner of the property, Rudolph Plegge, discovered the coveted spring waters while digging a well for himself in 1867. He quickly discovered he had a lucrative opportunity at his feet and began bottling and selling the mineral spring water. At the time mineral spring water was touted for its healing effects. After one woman drank the water and felt healed of her physical suffering, she begged her husband to buy the land so she'd never run out of the water. With the help of several cohorts, the woman's preacher husband purchased the land from Plegge and constructed a hotel on the site. People traveled from far and wide to stay at the hotel and swim in its mineral spring water pool. So many guests stayed there over the years that it should come as no surprise some of them now haunt the place. Hotel employees, especially, have observed countless incidents of paranormal activity. Ghostly figures have been spotted and their footsteps heard in the hallways, doors are opened and closed, and period music is sometimes heard playing throughout the hotel. Some of the most active places in the hotel include the laundry room, the balcony overlooking the mineral spring pool, and guestroom number 28, where a sad woman in white is said to haunt it. An explanation for some of the hauntings is the handful of disturbing deaths that have happened in the hotel. A former owner of the Original Mineral Springs Hotel, Tom Rogers, was found dead in one of the rooms on an upper floor, a guest named Conrad Paeben took his own life via suicide, and another guest, Ben Schierbaum, was murdered in 1916 when he was shot in the head.

Lakey's Creek

Among Little Egypt inhabitants the town of McLeansboro is known for a sinister legend closely resembling that of the Hessian headless horseman in Washington Irving's popular *Legend of Sleepy Hollow*. There is a narrow creek named for an early settler who built his cabin nearby. The little populated area didn't necessarily see many travelers in those days so no one knows exactly how long Lakey might have been sitting there, but one day a man passing through the area by wagon made a ghastly discovery. There, against the thick trunk of a tree, not far from the creek, sat the headless body of Mr. Lakey. Lakey's ax lay nearby and his head rested on the ground next to it. No one ever figured out who killed Mr. Lakey or why, but legend has it that Lakey now rides a steel black stallion along the creek in search of his killer. So be warned if you should choose to explore the creek because Lakey doesn't discriminate when it comes to selecting his next victim. And before you have a chance to become too skeptical, you might want to consider that an article appearing in the *Goshen Trails* periodical that was researched and written by Ralph S. Harrelson revealed that there was a real life Lakey. His name was actually Joel Leaky and he did live near the very creek that has come to be called Lakey's Creek. And, much like the man in the legend, Joel Leaky was also murdered — by his very own son-in-law! The real question now is whether this real life headless horseman inspired the classic story or if the story perpetuated the Lakey legend.

Claremont

Mount Pleasant Cemetery, located in Claremont, is a small and secluded cemetery that can be reached via a tree-lined drive near the intersection of Mount Pleasant Lane and Stringtown Road. The petite prairie like church that once hosted Sunday morning services still stands among the tombstones of its surrounding cemetery and is no bigger than a large shed. The small rectangular church has been boarded up and abandoned... for how long exactly is unknown. Nevertheless, it is the source of some interesting and eerie activity. Despite its boarded windows and doors and no clear means of entrance, strange sounds can be heard from within. The most common paranormal activity reported there includes a rapping at the front door, the sound of a choir singing inside, footsteps scuffling across the old plank floor, and a bright light shining through the tiny cracks in the wood of the boarded windows. There have even been sightings of phantom funerals in the surrounding church cemetery in recent years even though the last recorded funeral to take place there was in the 1950s.

Collinsville

Collinsville may be home to the world's largest catsup bottle, but it's also home to a few hauntings. Several of the town's most haunted hotspots have burned down, but paranormal activity is sometimes still detected at the sites of these former buildings. They include:

☠ Before it was reduced to ash, the Old First Baptist Church was haunted by seven different spirits, one of whom was the ghost of a janitor who died in the blaze that burnt down the church. Interestingly, the church caught fire in 2003 just a few days before the most haunted day of the year — Halloween.

☠ Another previously haunted building now gone due to fire was the mansion on Keebler Road. When the house was still standing, several witnesses reported seeing the ghosts of former slaves traveling from the large mansion to a nearby cemetery down the road.

☠ Elsewhere in town stands the haunted Miner's Theater, which is occupied by a playful female spirit who enjoys hiding the personal belongings of actors who perform there. Two ghostly brothers also haunt the place and can be heard fighting as they did in life when one killed the other.

But of all the interesting haunted sites in Collinsville, the most spiritual location is the impressive 2,200-acre Cahokia Mounds. The only pre-historic Indian city to still stand north of Mexico, the original people of the Cahokia area first settled there around 700 A.D. and remained until at least 1400 A.D. There were approximately 120 mounds total built up over time, and all were compiled by carrying heavy baskets full of dirt by hand from other locations to the site of the each mound. The Cahokia Mounds are considered to be the largest archeological site in the country and are a source of amazement for hundreds of visitors annually. But the mounds aren't the only sites to see in Cahokia. Some visitors have also spotted ghostly figures and spectral balls of light.

The Three Mile House

One of the most haunted sites in all of Little Egypt was a tavern and inn near Edwardsville known as the Three Mile House. The supernatural activity there was so intense that the property passed hands numerous times before burning down in 1985, which may have been for the best since it seems some of the spirits had gotten out of hand. All that remains of the Three Mile House today is an empty plot of grass speckled with some of the bricks that once formed the building. Even though the establishment no longer stands, some folks have speculated that its spirits are still there in their haunting form and have simply relocated to the St. James Cemetery directly across the street.

Construction on the Three Mile House began in 1858 and was finally completed in 1860. The building was said to have included several secret underground tunnels for use on the Underground Railroad. One of those tunnels may have even led to the cemetery across the street. Following years of operation, not just as an inn and tavern but also as a place for gambling, prostitution, and Prohibition era bootlegging, the establishment closed its doors and remained so for a quarter century until the Elliot family purchased it. It was at this time that the ghosts of the house really came out to play. Some of the activity included unexplained noises like tapping and knocking and the sound of the piano playing on its own. Objects were known to levitate while other items went missing. Dark shadowy apparitions were sometimes seen moving about the house—one of these figures was believed to be the spirit of an escaped slave named Tom who was murdered before he could achieve his freedom. Tom was a mischievous ghost who liked turning on the water in the bathrooms and kitchen until the rooms flooded—leaving a big mess for the Elliots.

The Elliot family soon became accustomed to their phantom friends and didn't mind them too much...until they started *scaring off* customers when a restaurant was opened in the building. The increasingly aggressive activity got to be too much for the staff to take as well. Eventually, after business dropped off, the Elliot family sold the Three Mile House and moved on to other things. The ghosts, however, remained. They lost their home, unfortunately, when the building was reduced to rubble after a fire consumed the entire estate. Now the ghosts are left only to haunt the secret tunnels that might still run beneath ground from the former foundation of the house to St. James Cemetery—or perhaps they've simply traveled *through* the tunnels and have relocated at the cemetery....

Cave-in-Rock State Park

Caves are great places for exploring, but they can also be dark and mysterious with tons of hidden secrets. One of the most intriguing caves in Southern Illinois is Cave-in-Rock, situated near the Ohio River in Cave-in-Rock State Park. The cave has even been featured in several movies, including "How the West was Won" starring John Wayne. The limestone cave is about fifty-five feet wide and two hundred feet long, large enough to provide shelter to weary travelers or serve as a hideout for criminals on the run. The cave's eclectic past includes such things as gambling, prostitution, counterfeiting, and murder.

Around 1797 river pirates led by Samuel Mason used to lure unsuspecting travelers to the cave with the promise of gambling, liquor, or prostitution inside. What better way to relax and unwind following a long trek down the river? Unfortunately, Mason's crew had other intentions that included robbing and killing these innocent travelers.

Mason and his pirate gang continued robbing and killing unsuspecting folks and were eventually joined by two cousins known as the Harpe Brothers, Big and Little Harpe. The Harpe Brothers made a career of killing men, women, and children from Virginia to Kentucky and are considered by some to be the first American serial killers. At one point, the Harpe Brothers made their way to Illinois and met up with the infamous Sam Mason and his gang. Big and Little Harpe joined Mason and his crew in the cave, attacking travelers along the river. At some point, Mason's crew had enough when the Harpe Brothers tied a man to his horse, blindfolded the horse, and sent the man and horse off a cliff to their deaths below. Even by pirate standards, the Harpe Brothers had gone too far and were kicked out of the cave and the gang. That wasn't the end of the Harpes though. Sometime later Little Harpe returned with another outlaw and killed Mason in order to collect the bounty on his head. Eventually justice caught up with both Harpes and they were killed.

It should be no surprise then that, with the cave's bloody history, it's now haunted by the spirits of many of the unsuspecting victims who lost their lives at the hands of the Mason gang or the Harpe Brothers. Perhaps even Mason himself haunts the cave. Visitors of the state park sometimes report hearing ghostly moans and cries coming from inside the cave. For those brave enough to venture inside, there is also a distinctly eerie feeling that pervades the interior. The cave is certainly a spectacular sight...just don't be surprised by the spooky sounds you hear.

The Ghosts of Grafton

Just beyond the invisible boundary of Little Egypt at its northwestern edge near Alton lies the tiny town of Grafton. It sits on the riverfront right at the point where the Mississippi, Missouri, and Illinois rivers flow into one another. This area is often referred to as the Meeting of the Great Rivers Scenic Byway and is known for its limestone bluffs, thick forests, and extensive wildlife. Ferries travel the river waters from one town to the next. In days gone by, steamboats could be seen chugging along, transporting travelers and goods to various riverfront destinations.

Grafton has long been a part of Southern Illinois' history with early settlements first popping up around 1812. The town of Grafton itself was officially established in 1832. In all those years, the town certainly built up quite an extensive history, some traces of which persist today in the lingering spirits and haunting of the Grafton area and the Great River Road that runs through it.

Some of the most notable haunted spots in Grafton include:

- Ruebel Hotel
- River House
- Grafton Boatworks
- Loading Dock Bar and Grill
- An area known as Baby Hollow

Some of these locations still stand today; others have changed face or disappeared completely over the years. Many of these haunted places can be reached via the Great River Road as it follows the twists and turns of the winding river.

Of the numerous Grafton ghost stories, the place purported to be the most haunted is Ruebel Hotel located on Main Street. The hotel was originally built in 1884 by Michael Ruebel and enjoyed a successful run for several years catering to travelers along the river until business slowed with the advent of the Great Depression in the 1930s. The hotel eventually closed and remained empty for several decades before its legacy would finally be preserved through restoration efforts. The hotel later reopened in 1997. To the surprise of many of the hotel's new guests, they soon discovered that many of its former ones had never checked out. In all the years the hotel was seemingly abandoned, turns out there may have been some unexpected residents inside all along. With the reopening of the hotel, strange sounds and spectral sightings were enough to convince many that it was haunted. One ghost is especially familiar to hotel guests and staff: the ghost of a young girl named Abigail is regularly seen playing at the top of the stairway leading to the second floor, as well as in an upstairs hallway. It's unclear what fate led her to take up permanent residency in the long-standing hotel, but she is well known and welcomed around the hotel.

Besides Ruebel Hotel, the River House, a popular tavern among miscreants, used to be touted as another extremely haunted location before it was torn down. The infamous River House came to be known as the Bloody Bucket for all the violence and many murders that occurred on the premises. Reportedly, when the place was finally demolished, blood spatter was discovered all over the interior walls...accompanied by a still hanging noose. Before the tavern's demise, people used to report hearing the sounds of ghosts walking about. The ghosts, most likely, are the restless spirits of tavern patrons who died as a result of bar fights, brawls, and cold-blooded murder.

The River House may be long gone, but the Grafton Boatworks and nearby Loading Dock Bar & Grill still stand and are both said to be haunted by the spirits of former Boatworks employees whose phantom footsteps can sometimes be heard pacing the floors as the men scurry to complete paddle wheelers, barges, and military gunboats. No one is sure of the identities of any of these ghostly men or the reason they continue working after all these years, but hearing the unmistakable sound of metal being molded into ship parts as the men scuffle about is sign enough that they're still around.

Other spirit activity can be observed in a wooded area of Grafton known as Baby Hollow. The spirits of early Grafton citizens are believed to haunt the woods; these are citizens who fell ill with smallpox and other diseases and who were sent to a secluded building in the woods known as the Pest House. Most of these people never recovered and died while under quarantine in the house. Their bodies were typically buried in the surrounding woods. Even though the Pest House was leveled long ago, the spirits of the deceased ill are still heard crying and weeping in despair throughout Baby Hollow.

If you dig around a little, you may uncover even more ghosts and hauntings around Grafton. After all, countless people have passed through the riverfront town over the years and there are bound to be some remnants of the past still lurking where you least expect. Once you've explored all the haunted hotspots in Grafton, you might try taking a trip down the Great River Road on your way to Alton where additional haunts await.

☠☠☠☠☠

2

Alton

Alton

The small town of Alton sits along the Mississippi River in the southwestern portion of the state where the river forms a natural border between Illinois and Missouri. Many folks consider Alton to be one of the most haunted small towns in America. A look back at its history shows that the happenings there over time certainly lend themselves to ghosts and hauntings. In particular, Alton's location just on the other side of the river from St. Louis made it a logical spot for several stations on the Underground Railroad. Unfortunately, the sad reality of the Underground Railroad is that many individuals died before freedom was realized due to poor health, cold conditions, and malnourishment. It wasn't always easy to stay strong and healthy while on the run. Many escaped slaves died along the journey.

It was certainly a sad time in our history in some ways, the evidence of which can still be observed in the secret passageways running beneath many homes and buildings in Alton, as well as in other nearby areas. Many believe the spirits of escaped slaves who passed away before having the chance to fully embrace their newfound freedom continue to remain trapped in the tunnels, forever haunting these sites. And then there were those who died fighting for that freedom, such as the Reverend Elijah Lovejoy who was murdered for his abolitionist views. His spirit is said to still wander, and so our journey through Alton begins with him.

The Spirit of Abolitionist Elijah Parish Lovejoy

A fiery scene lit up the dark night sky as an angry mob surrounded an old warehouse along the Mississippi River. They set the building ablaze hoping to force out an enemy who had taken refuge inside. The violent mob must have been out for blood that night because they came armed with rifles and loathing. Amidst the burning building, gunshots, and violence someone would soon die beneath that cold November night sky.

Back before the Civil War pitted north against south, tensions were already running high between states supporting slavery and those opposing it. For instance, both Illinois and Missouri shared a border, but socially and politically they were at odds. While Missouri was a slave state, Illinois was a free one.

Living and working in Illinois, however, was not enough to isolate a person from anti-abolitionist sentiments. One of the most notable examples of this was the persistent persecution of the very vocal slavery abolitionist Elijah Parish Lovejoy. Lovejoy was a journalist who left Missouri after being harshly criticized for his anti-slavery views. He moved to Illinois hoping to enjoy true freedom of speech and freedom of the press. Unfortunately, he would find neither.

Lovejoy moved from Maine to St. Louis, Missouri in 1826. He established a school in St. Louis before eventually attending seminary and becoming a minister. While serving as the pastor of a local church, Lovejoy started a newspaper called the *St. Louis Observer*. The views expressed in that paper would ultimately get him into serious trouble, even putting his life in jeopardy.

Reverend Lovejoy's *St. Louis Observer* was a religious paper that promoted the abolition of slavery, and angered many a Missourian. Lovejoy managed to continue printing and distributing his controversial newspaper for a good two years before some locals had enough and decided to retaliate. They destroyed the printing press he used to publish the *St. Louis Observer* so that he could no longer distribute his offensive views in print. In order to continue freely printing and publishing, Lovejoy sought solace on the Illinois side of the Mississippi.

So what did Lovejoy do that was bad enough to be forced out of St. Louis, Missouri?

Well, he spoke out against the lynching of a black man named Frank McIntosh. The mistreatment of blacks in slave states at the time was not uncommon. However, Frank McIntosh was not a slave. He was black and, free or not, that was enough for trouble to find him in antebellum America. McIntosh had previously been held as a murder suspect, and even spent some time in jail for it. Regardless of the fact that he was still innocent until proven guilty, an angry mob took the law into their own hands and lynched McIntosh. When a judge essentially acquitted everyone involved, Reverend Lovejoy was incensed and immediately published an article condemning them, including the ironically named judge, Luke Lawless. The article didn't go over well with St. Louis locals who ultimately came after Lovejoy and destroyed his printing press. Not surprisingly, the individuals responsible for destroying the press were likely the same ones who had also been involved in the McIntosh lynching.

Lovejoy would not be deterred. He was intent on exercising his right to free speech, but he wasn't crazy. He took a hint, left Missouri, and headed across the Mississippi River where he relocated in Alton, Illinois. In Alton, Lovejoy set up shop once again and began printing the *Alton Observer*. Unfortunately, his troubles weren't over. As long as Lovejoy continued publishing anti-slavery articles, he would have enemies.

Three times, Lovejoy's printing presses were confiscated and tossed into the nearby Mississippi River to prevent him from printing his anti-slavery views. Each time a press was tossed into the muddy waters of the Mississippi, Lovejoy managed to obtain a new one and continued printing and publishing. The arrival of his fourth replacement press would mark the beginning of the end, or so it would seem.

On a chilly November night, hours after most folks had long been sleeping, a sturdy steamboat chugged its way quietly along the smooth waters of the Mississippi. The steamboat carried a brand new printing press toward Alton while Elijah Lovejoy and company awaited its arrival inside the Godfrey, Gilman, & Company warehouse. The printing press was delivered around three o'clock in the morning, but despite the late hour its arrival didn't go unnoticed. A hostile mob assembled, already aware of the clandestine delivery, and began to make its way toward the warehouse demanding that the press be turned over to them. When Lovejoy and his supporters refused, the mob took action.

Before long, the roof of the warehouse had been set ablaze. Rifle shots were aimed through windows at Lovejoy and the other occupants inside while unarmed mobsters contributed to the chaos by throwing stones. Lovejoy and his group attempted to defend themselves and the new printing press, but ultimately they were no match for the charged mob. Several individuals were shot, including Lovejoy. The rest surrendered themselves and the printing press, which was subsequently smashed to bits and tossed into the river. But the destruction of the press would be only a minor loss. The real tragedy would be the death of Reverend Elijah Lovejoy who would not survive the fatal gunshot wound he suffered that night.

Hours after Lovejoy's friends and supporters would surrender the printing press and, themselves, abandon the warehouse, his body would remain at the site of his murder throughout that fateful night while the building continued to burn around him. Meanwhile, the mob celebrated their victory. When Lovejoy's body was finally taken away the following day and carried down the street toward his home, members of the ruthless mob cheered and laughed at his death. Ironically, Lovejoy would be laid to rest on the day of his birth, November 9, 1837. He would have been thirty-five years old.

Despite the continued destruction of Lovejoy's printing presses, he would not be silenced and continued to promote the abolition of slavery. Only in death could his enemies finally quiet him, or could they? Since that fateful November night, there have been countless reports of unexplained activity around the area along the Mississippi River, where the warehouse once stood as a symbol of free speech and freethinking. There is an unidentified but intense energy that is experienced by anyone who visits the site. The determined slave-supporting mob may have been able to take his printing press, and even his life, but they couldn't quell Lovejoy's fierce spirit. He continues to roam the riverside accompanied by the crazed energy that filled the air the night he died. Even though it all happened more than one hundred years ago, Lovejoy's restless spirit seems to linger, haunting the area near the Mississippi River into which his printing presses were thrown and an empty area between two large grain mills where the old printing warehouse used to stand before being burned that night.

Alton Cemetery

The spirit of Elijah Lovejoy not only wanders the banks of the Mississippi River near where he lost his life in the name of freedom, but also the cemetery where he was buried. Alton Cemetery is located on Monument Avenue and bears a tributary monument dedicated to Reverend Lovejoy. The granite monument stands tall atop a set of stone steps and sports a brilliant bronze statue of the winged angel of Victory. On either side of the ninety-three feet tall commemorative column are two shorter granite pillars each bearing a bronze eagle with wings outstretched. Several inscriptions are posted around the monument, which was originally dedicated on the anniversary of Lovejoy's death in 1897 and then again in a rededication ceremony in 1969. Lovejoy must be pleased with the monument because, on occasion, his spirit can be seen in its vicinity. Visiting admirers have also reported random and uncharacteristic cold spots near the monument when the surrounding temperature is much warmer.

However, Elijah Lovejoy isn't the only spectral image seen in the Alton Cemetery—the ghost of a young girl named Lucy Haskell has also been spotted roaming the cemetery grounds.

Little Lucy was just nine years old when she died in 1890 from the disease Diphtheria. Lucy is still remembered around Alton at least once a year when a birthday party is thrown in her honor every July near the Lucy Haskell Playhouse in Haskell Park. Lucy's grandfather John Hayner had a beautiful 224-square foot playhouse with stained glass windows built a few years before she died. The playhouse still stands in Haskell Park today. No one really knows if little Lucy Haskell's spirit ever joins the annual festivities at her former playhouse, but she is known to wander Alton Cemetery near the Hayner and Haskell Monument where she is buried.

There is also another haunting in the cemetery around the Grandview Mausoleum. It seems someone here is not at rest. A phantom woman dressed all in black is sometimes seen walking near the otherwise quiet mausoleum. The woman has yet to be identified and no one knows why she wanders rather than rest in peace. Perhaps when those questions can be answered the woman will finally find what she's looking for.

Spirits & Suicide at First Unitarian Church

The Reverend Elijah Lovejoy seems to be everywhere in Alton. While he does not haunt the place, he does have a connection with another of Alton's most haunted locations. When Lovejoy was still alive, he was friends with the Reverend Charles Farley, who was the pastor of First Unitarian Church, one of Alton's haunted hotspots. The church began as a small group called the First Unitarian Society. The society was established by the grandfather of renowned poet and playwright T. S. Eliot around 1836. At the time, there was not much acceptance of the church by folks in Alton. The predominantly Catholic town was not especially receptive to the unfamiliar Unitarian Society. This lack of acceptance extended to Reverend Farley when it was strongly suggested that he leave town following the murder of his dear friend Elijah Lovejoy if he didn't want to also suffer the same fate. Farley didn't need to be told twice, as he quickly left Alton.

Following Reverend Farley's departure, the First Unitarian Society was left without a leader as well as a permanent address. Up to that point the congregation had simply been meeting in various homes. It was time to build an actual brick and mortar church. In 1905 a site was selected on the corner of Third and Alby streets where a Catholic church had previously stood before burning down and being rebuilt elsewhere. The original foundation remained intact despite its fire ravaged appearance and the new Unitarian Church was constructed right over this existing foundation. Interestingly, it's believed that the previous church building may have once been utilized as a safe haven on the Underground Railroad. A series of unusual tunnels and passageways still exist beneath the Unitarian Church today.

After the new church building was completed, several pastors came and went over the years, but there is one who has never left. Although he is no longer seen in the flesh, his footsteps can still be heard walking through the sanctuary and throughout the building as he locks and unlocks various doors. Sometimes his presence can even be felt, literally. Church members have reported feeling a slight push or touch from an invisible source on occasion. Many also experience an eerie feeling downstairs in the basement where the tunnels of the Underground Railroad lie. Strange odors have also been detected at times. So who is this spirit that haunts First Unitarian Church?

Reverend Phillip Mercer came to Alton and First Unitarian Church in 1928. He was well liked among the congregation, but was an extremely private individual, never sharing much about his personal life prior to Alton. Mercer served the church for six years before the mysteriousness that surrounded his life would culminate in his untimely death. On a late November afternoon in 1934, the body of Reverend Mercer was discovered hanging from a beam overhead with a sash around the neck and a chair nearby. The good reverend had apparently committed suicide.

Mercer's death would soon become enshrouded in as much mystery as his life had been. There was no clear explanation as to why Mercer would have taken his own life. He had not left a suicide note and everyone was at a loss as to why he would have done it. Those closest to him did recall noticing some recent changes in Mercer prior to his passing. He had gone on a trip and upon returning to Alton he seemed to have grown increasingly concerned with his eating habits. He had developed an intense focus on losing weight and showed signs of severe mood swings as he began to lose weight quickly. Some of his good friends expressed concern that he might have been suffering the onset of a nervous breakdown just prior to his suicide. There was no clear answer to explain the tragic event, however, a surprise acquaintance would reveal additional information about Mercer that was previously unknown to anyone in his congregation. A woman from Minnesota, Dorothy Cole, who had known Mercer before he ever set foot in Alton, shared with Mercer's friends that he had been extremely depressed for quite a long time. He had been effective at hiding the depression from his friends and parishioners, but the unexpected suicide was a pretty good indication that something had been seriously wrong. An even bigger surprise still was the announcement that Mercer had been engaged to Dorothy and was planning to marry her. This news took everyone by surprise as he had never even mentioned any romantic involvement.

The body of Phillip Mercer was laid to rest within the confines of the Grandview Mausoleum at Alton Cemetery. His death left several questions unanswered, which might be the reason Mercer seems compelled to haunt his old church rather than rest in eternal peace. Mercer's ghost can often be seen in the area near his old study where he hung himself. His presence has also been felt in the sanctuary where he used to deliver sermons on Sunday mornings. There are even times when church staff members arrive early to open up the church only to discover Mercer has already unlocked the doors for them as though he's simply awaiting their arrival. Others have even felt something supernatural down in the church basement, but it isn't necessarily the spirit of Phillip Mercer. There just might be a few spirits of escaped pre-Civil War slaves still wandering the secret underground passageways to freedom.

So far as anyone can tell Mercer's spirit is harmless and isn't really out to scare anyone. As for the energies in the basement, no one is sure quite what to think. Regardless, most folks prefer not to be left alone for too long in any part of the church because, the truth is, you're never really alone inside First Unitarian Church.

Alton Penitentiary

Two and a half decades following the violent death of abolitionist Elijah Lovejoy in 1837, the stage was set for the Civil War. Calamity broke out in 1861 when the pro-slavery Confederates of the south descended upon Fort Sumpter, a government military base, in South Carolina proclaiming their succession from the Union. As war raged on for the next four years, soldiers were killed and captured on either side. For the Union, they needed a place to secure Confederate prisoners. Alton had its own military base at the time; however, existing military facilities had become overcrowded. A request was made to utilize the Alton Penitentiary to house Confederate prisoners. The prison was empty at the time and the request was granted.

Built in 1833, Alton Penitentiary was the first state-operated prison in Illinois. Previously, convicts were typically locked up in local jails throughout the state. And there would be no federal institutions until 1895 when the United States Government first opened the Leavenworth facility in Kansas on the site of a prior military prison. Alton Penitentiary remained in operation as a state facility until 1860 when it closed following the opening of the Joliet Correctional Center in 1858. Many Alton prisoners were then transferred to Joliet to finish their sentences and the prison was left standing empty. All that remains of the original prison today is a portion of gray stonewall near a park located at the corner of Broadway and Williams Street.

During the time when the facility functioned as a military prison, there were many deaths. Confederate inmates struggled with maltreatment, poor hygiene, inadequate clothing, and deadly disease. It was a miracle any of them survived confinement there. The worst culprit of all was an outbreak of the smallpox virus in 1863. Not only did the unstoppable disease wipeout a good portion of the inmate population, but many prison guards also contracted the disease and died as well. Infected prison staff even spread the disease among family and friends throughout the city of Alton before realizing they were ill. The epidemic became so problematic within the confines of the prison that the decision was made to quarantine many of the sick prisoners on a secluded island across the Mississippi River. The tiny island was then known as Sunflower Island, but was soon dubbed Smallpox Island after countless infected individuals died there after a losing battle with the disease. The dead were buried both on the island and along the nearby Missouri shoreline. Unfortunately, they would not be able to rest in complete peace when the muddy waters of the Mississippi River slowly eroded the tiny island over time. Some of the once buried bodies were eventually dislodged and washed away downstream where they were later discovered. The previously smallpox plagued island is now believed to be inhabited by the spirits of the deadly disease's victims, as is the area where Alton Penitentiary once stood overlooking the city on one side and the might river on the other.

After the cessation of the war, the prison was once again closed down and abandoned. By 1870 many of the former prison buildings had even been torn down. The sturdy gray stones that had once formed the walls of the giant prison were pulled apart and reused in new construction efforts around Alton. Some were even used to build a brand new railway bridge. Although the prison no longer stands today, a small slice of this turbulent time has been preserved. A memorial plaque commemorating all the lives lost during the Civil War marks the corner piece of wall that can be found near Broadway and Williams Street. But don't think that just because a parking lot now sits where the prison once stood, there aren't any Confederate ghosts still haunting the area. From time to time the ghosts of Confederate soldiers can be seen lingering in the area where they were once imprisoned. And even before the prison was completely torn down and simply stood empty and ominous, people visiting the nearby park often reported hearing unexplained voices and cries emanating from inside the vacant prison walls.

Hop Hollow Road

The ghosts of captured Confederate soldiers don't just lurk near the site of the old Alton Penitentiary. Uniformed Confederate apparitions are sometimes also seen wandering along a dark wooded stretch of road on Rozier Street near what was once old Hop Hollow Road. Before the Alton Penitentiary smallpox epidemic created an overflow of bodies needing burying, Confederate soldiers who died in custody were originally transported along the Mississippi River by ferry to a small cemetery on Rozier Street. When the ferry docked at its destination, Union soldiers were responsible for transferring the bodies to a wagon and transporting them to the secluded cemetery via a winding wooded path known as Hop Hollow Road. The deceased Confederate soldiers were to be properly prepared for burial only they didn't always make it to the cemetery. Legend has it that rather than make the long trek through the woods along Hop Hollow Road, Union soldiers sometimes buried their Confederate counterparts in the nearby woods.

Today Hop Hollow Road is little more than a desolate trail on predominantly private property. According to police records, several years ago a group of teens discovered some old bones back in the woods where they were presumably trespassing while hanging out and goofing around. Turns out, the bones may have been the remains of various Confederate soldiers who were hastily buried in the woods rather than properly placed in the nearby cemetery as was intended. In time additional bones were discovered in the area as well, along with miscellaneous items that would indicate the bodies had indeed been there since the Civil War. Subsequent to the unearthing of the old bones there have been several sightings of peculiar hitchhikers looking a bit disheveled and dressed in ragged old military uniforms attempting to wave down a ride. Perhaps these Confederate ghosts are hoping to hitch their way to the cemetery where they belong. I wouldn't recommend picking them up, though, should you ever encounter these phantom soldiers along old Hop Hollow Road.

The Enos Building

The Enos building on Third Street in Alton was also previously known as the Nathanial Hanson Mansion. The large home was built for Nathanial Hanson in 1857 and included several secret tunnels and rooms beneath the house that would become part of the Underground Railroad. Hanson was firmly against slavery and hoped to do whatever he could to assist slaves in finding freedom. In addition to the secret refuge beneath the house, Hanson also had a small tower constructed on the roof from which he could signal across the Mississippi River when the coast was clear for escaped slaves to cross from Missouri to Illinois. Reportedly, a light was flashed from the tower once for the all clear and twice when danger loomed. Hanson was able to assist many people in their quest for freedom, but some died along their journey and their spirits may still be attached to the Hanson Mansion. Remnants of the covert Underground Railroad can still be observed beneath the house, although many of the passages and rooms have since been bricked off.

Sometime after the Civil War, the mansion was sold to a doctor by the name of Enos, who converted the place into a long-term care hospital for tuberculosis patients. Dr. Enos added onto the already large building in order to accommodate the increasing numbers of infected individuals. He hoped to provide an environment in which his patients could bask in the fresh air on their road to recovery. Unfortunately, the seriousness of the disease meant that many of the patients ultimately died and would never leave Enos' hospital. Instead, they passed away in a place that would become a permanent home to many...as some of the former patients are believed to now haunt the upper floors of the old hospital.

The building was eventually converted into apartments, but when new tenants began moving in they would soon discover they had gotten more than they bargained for. The basement area and its attached tunnels seemed to be infested with paranormal activity, as did different areas on the upper floors. Over the years various residents of the building have reported hearing strange sounds that cannot be attributed to any earthly explanation, including phantom footsteps and pained cries. Additionally, lights often turn themselves on and off while doors open and close independently. Personal effects sometimes go missing for several days before mysteriously popping up again in another location. Perhaps the strangest tale is the repeated occurrence of scratching sounds at a door leading to the basement in one of the first floor apartments. Various occupants of the apartment over the years have reported hearing the bizarre scratching noises. They sounded as if someone were trapped below trying to claw their way out or signal for help. Even more disturbing was that each time anyone opened the basement door to have a look there was never anyone there. Between the spirits of escaped slaves trapped in the basement and those of tuberculosis patients roaming the halls on the upper floors of the building, the Enos Apartments are truly an unsettling place to live.

The Kendall Cracker Factory

Alton has long been known for its antique shops with beautiful treasures of old. But the antiques inside the shops aren't the only things from yesteryear. Some say the ghosts of individuals from days gone by still wander through the shops. One building in particular—known as the Cracker Factory—is especially haunted. Many believe the main ghost in the building to be that of a man named Sam Thames who once owned it. Thames acquired the building in 1972 and worked to build up the budding antique business in Alton. His goal was to attract antique collectors from everywhere, not just locals from Alton and surrounding towns.

Sam Thames took a lot of pride in developing a prosperous antique district. It all began when he set up his own antique store in the basement of the old Kendall Steam Cracker Factory. The multi-story building had plenty of space for several antique stores and other businesses, but Thames chose a most unusual location for his own shop. When the Cracker Factory was still in operation, the hundreds of crackers and biscuits that were churned out each day were baked downstairs in the basement. There sat five sturdy ovens capable of producing up to 150 barrels of biscuits and crackers a day. Kendall Cracker Factory products were distributed for sale throughout Alton. The building was originally constructed specifically for the Cracker Factory in 1866 and was named for its owner, Hiram Kendall. The main floor of the building served as a storefront, where the popular baked goods produced right downstairs could be sold fresh out of the oven. The upper floors of the building accommodated the offices of Hiram Kendall and his associates. Over the years the cracker business passed hands several times, first to Daniels, Bayle, & Company and then to the Schnell G. F. Baking company. The building was later bought by a man named Henry McPike sometime during the 1890s—and, as you'll discover a little later, Henry McPike is known to haunt another infamous site in Alton.

Sam Thames eventually owned the building from 1972 to 1994. He set up shop down in the basement and leased out space on the main floor so that the entire building was soon full of different antique shops. Up on the third floor, Sam had a loft apartment where he lived—and later died from pancreatic cancer in 1994. Following Thames' death many of the shops closed or relocated and the building soon stood empty. Although many believe Thames was still attached to the place, they didn't know for sure until other businesses began to occupy the old Cracker Factory once again. As new businesses opened up shop throughout the building, many of the owners and employees began to see and hear strange things, such as phantom footsteps and unexplained whistling. Many folks believe one of the ghosts residing in the Cracker Factory to be that of Sam Thames himself. Others believe he isn't the only spirit to haunt the building. In fact, ghosts are said to have wandered the factory even when Sam Thames was still alive.

The spirits don't seem to mean any harm, though. Thames' ghost may even be trying to lend a helping hand. He is known to flip the "closed" sign around to "open" first thing in the morning before the owners arrive for the day. During the frigid winter months, the heat is often already turned up to a comfortable temperature when shopkeepers arrive in the morning despite having been turned down to a much lower setting the night before. Such activity was especially common in the Riverbend Treasures shop that has occupied the basement space since 2002 where Thames used to keep shop. Before the store converted to online operations exclusively, strange things used to take place in the legendary basement location. Items were sometimes moved around overnight, the normally in-sync radios would all be switched to different stations, and the unmistakable odor of burning biscuits occasionally wafted from the oven area where three of the original five antique cracker ovens still stand. And it wasn't unheard of for customers to sometimes feel an invisible force brush against them while perusing the antique store. Icy cold spots were not uncommon either. There's been a lot of strange activity happening at the Kendall Cracker Factory over the years and it looks like it will continue for years to come.

McPike Mansion

After the Kendall Steam Cracker Factory business was long gone from Alton, the building that had once been its home came under the ownership of a man named Henry McPike who leased out portions of it to various businesses. Henry McPike was a prosperous Alton business man who became widely known in the area for the McPike grape, a large grape grown locally on the McPike property. The McPike family lived in a large mansion on Alby Street from about 1869 to 1936. The three-story tall home and its sprawling estate was one of the most impressive in all of Alton. There was even a wine cellar in the basement, perhaps where the McPike's produced their own wine from McPike grapes.

The mansion went on to have several different owners following the McPikes, including a man named Paul Laichinger, who rented several of the rooms out to other individuals. The house was eventually abandoned and, in the absence of proper upkeep, soon deteriorated. The house is now owned by the Luedke family, although they don't live there themselves. In fact, no one has lived in the house since the 1950s due to its structurally unsafe condition. The Luedkes purchased the building in 1994 and have slowly been renovating it over the years with the hope of someday returning the mansion to its former glory. Since the Luedkes have owned the house, they've had numerous ghostly encounters. Perhaps the dilapidated condition of the house doesn't sit well with whatever spirits might be there or maybe all the recent restoration efforts have roused previously dormant energies. Whatever the cause, there has been extensive supernatural activity documented at the mansion by both paranormal investigators and psychics. Much of this activity has also been witnessed by countless visitors, as well as the Luedkes themselves.

Some of the many spirits said to haunt the old McPike Mansion include Henry McPike, his wife, their servant Sarah Wells, and even Paul Laichinger. McPike's spirit is said to be especially hostile toward women and it's believed he used to aggressively punish his wife and female servants if they were ever out of line. One investigator was reportedly even slapped across the face by McPike's invisible hand. Despite his controlling tendencies, one of his former servants seems to have found some solace in the afterlife. The spirit of Sarah Wells, a former servant of the house, is regularly detected on the third floor where the scent of lilacs wafts through the air. From outside on the grounds, she can often be seen looking out an upstairs window as well. This mischievous spirit is known to temporarily hide personal effects, such as jewelry and other small items, as if to intentionally make her presence known.

Miss Sarah Wells isn't the only ghost to peek out through the windows of the upper floors. Numerous eyewitnesses have also spotted a man looking out one of the upstairs windows. When shown several photos of various individuals matching the description of the man, the anonymous specter was soon identified as Paul Laichinger, one of the former owners of the property post the McPike family era. The ghostly images of both Sarah Wells and Paul Laichinger have been captured in photos of the building's exterior. Other unexpected surprises have also been revealed in different photos of the mansion, including unexplained balls of light. And an investigation of the wine cellar even resulted in the appearance of a strange lilac colored mist on video. For a long time now the McPike Mansion has been host to a plethora of paranormal activity and you can check it out for yourself by signing up for one of the many tours conducted throughout the year.

The Boothby Mansion House

There's an old apartment building located on State Street dating back to 1834 that is often referred to as the Mansion House. With a grand name like that, the place would seem to be a renter's dream, but for many it's the stuff of nightmares. Unusual noises often emanate throughout the building, not the least of which are horrific blood-curdling screams sometimes heard in the middle of the night seemingly coming from a corner apartment. Tenants in other apartments around the building might mistake the screams as evidence of a violent assault happening behind closed doors. Imagine their surprise at finding out that the screams are not of this world. Scarier yet, imagine living in that corner apartment and hearing the bloody screams first hand... *night after night*.

That's not such a far-fetched thing. More than a century ago, when the building first operated as a hotel, guests spent many a sleepless night trying to block out the sounds of a hysterical man ravaged by madness and obsession. In 1836 a man named Tom Boothby rented a corner room from Captain Botkin, the hotel's owner. Boothby resided in the hotel for the next two years. Other guests may have stayed there just as long were it not for Boothby's antics. Boothby was a recluse and spent most of the time locked away alone in his room. He reportedly even had someone bring his meals to his room so that he wouldn't have to leave even to eat. Boothby had established quite a strange reputation around the hotel and soon became notorious among guests for his terrible night terrors from which he'd wake up screaming. Needless to say, most guests found it difficult to get a decent night's sleep with Boothby screaming nearby and didn't necessarily stick around for very long after that.

So what could have caused Boothby's night terrors? Was his room haunted? Did he wake to find evil apparitions hovering over him? Apparently, Tom Boothby had previously killed countless Indians while fighting in the War of 1812. It seems he feared they would one day take their revenge on him and used to have recurring nightmares about it. This went on for the duration of his two-year stay at the hotel until he was discovered one morning dead in his room. When Boothby didn't respond to a food tray being left for him as usual, everyone knew something was wrong. Captain Botkin retrieved the key to unlock Boothby's room, but upon opening the door he saw a truly strange sight. There was Boothby laying dead across the bed, shirt torn, and a look of fear upon his face. Even more startling was his own hand gripped tightly around his throat in a choke hold. Was Boothby trying to stop a phantom assault in the middle of the night or had he choked himself to death? Whatever the real answer, there's no doubt Boothby must have believed Indians had truly come to avenge the death of their cohorts. Too bad for Boothby he wasn't able to finally find peace in death. His frightened cries can still be heard coming from within the corner apartment where his old room used to be inside the Mansion House and are enough to terrify current tenants right out of there.

Hartford Castle

When it still stood proudly in the small Hartford community of Alton near Cahokia Creek, the Hartford Castle was a breathtaking sight. At the time, the estate was called Lakeview and belonged to the Biszant family. The mansion-sized house was surrounded by acres of wooded land adorned with gardens, gazebos, statues, and lakes. Throughout the property, the sound of soft music could often be heard playing from within the house. Benjamin Biszant had the large home built for his wife in 1897. Unfortunately, his wife was able to only enjoy her beautiful dream home for a short time. She passed away within a few years of living in the house. The heartbroken Biszant sold the house and moved away. The house had a handful of owners in the years that followed, and was even used as a speakeasy for a time when it was a resort. There, people were free to purchase and consume alcohol in secret during the relatively short-lived Prohibition era. Speakeasies were named for the implication that it was necessary to speak "easy," or speak softly, so as not to rouse the attention of law enforcement or snitches regarding the illicit alcohol consumption taking place inside. As far as Hartford Castle goes, business carried on as usual for many years, but in time the house was eventually left standing empty. With no one to maintain the large estate, the house and grounds quickly decayed and was no longer recognizable as the grand mansion it had once been.

After the house had been abandoned and left to nature, curiosity seekers began exploring the property. What they would discover was completely unexpected. On several occasions the ghostly figure of a woman was seen wandering the overgrown grounds of her once lush yard. She is sometimes heard crying, and other times classical music is heard coming from an unknown source off in the distance of the secluded property. Interestingly, the house burned down in 1973...yet *sightings* of the distressed woman continue on the property, as does the playing of the unexplained phantom music. Many people believe this restless spirit to be that of Biszant's wife, forever attached to the glorious home he had so lovingly built as a gift to her.

Mineral Springs Hotel

Mineral Springs Hotel was built in 1914 and saw all sorts of guests over the years—many of whom have never left the building. Ghostly sightings have included a struggling artist who likes to linger near the old hotel bar and an angry husband who appears near the pool where he fell in and drowned during an argument with his wife. Some individuals refute these stories, suggesting they are the products of urban legend. Still, others claim to have actually *seen* these apparitions in person, both near the hotel pool and bar.

Perhaps the most popular paranormal story associated with Mineral Springs Hotel concerns an apparition known as the Jasmine Lady. No one is sure who she was in life, but in death, she's easily identified by the distinct scent of jasmine so strong that it's almost too much to bear. Her presence is often accompanied by sudden cold temperatures in the immediate area as well. She has even been bold enough to reach out and touch certain people. The elegant Jasmine Lady is most often seen near a staircase where it's believed she lost her life when she tripped down the steps and broke her neck. Some people believe the fall to have been an accident, others aren't so sure. They insist she was pushed down the stairs by her jealous husband after he caught her with another man. In some accounts, realizing what he had done, her distraught husband went up to their room and killed himself. Whichever way it happened, the Jasmine Lady seems to have met her demise on the stairway. Consequently, she now continues to travel up and down the stairs...and may very well do so for eternity.

Finally, one of the most interesting ghostly encounters at the hotel, as told by ghost investigator Troy Taylor, occurred several years after the building had been remodeled to accommodate various shops, restaurants, and businesses. An employee at the time was working in an area downstairs near one of the old mineral spring pools when he heard the sound of water. The pool, which was closed off and locked up, had not been used in years. And it certainly wasn't filled with water anymore. Something wasn't right so the perplexed employee decided to unlock the door to the pool and take a look. Upon opening the door everything looked to be in order at first glance. Perhaps the employee had only heard the sound of the mineral spring's rushing water flowing in the ground beneath him. Even though the mineral springs were no longer used in association with the former hotel, they still flowed freely underground. That was a logical explanation for the noise, but it didn't explain what the employee saw next. A series of wet footprints ran along the walk surrounding the pool as though a swimmer had just stepped out of the water. The footprints continued for several feet before abruptly stopping. It was as if whoever had walked there had simply disappeared into thin air. Either that or their feet had completely dried before exiting the pool area. Yet there was *no one* in sight. That was enough to scare the employee away, never to return to the old pool area again. Other apparitions have also been spotted by employees of the various establishments in the building over the years. There are often unidentified people seen wandering around, but whenever anyone attempts to follow these mysterious individuals, they can never be traced...as they always seem to vanish into thin air.

The Hotel's History

The hotel's history is as interesting as its hauntings. Originally planned as an ice plant, two brothers named Herman and August Luer began construction in 1910. They already owned a successful meat packing plant in the area and were excited to be expanding their business. As construction efforts got underway, workers soon unearthed a mineral spring underground. The meat-packing Luer brothers were advised to take advantage of the natural spring that flowed on their property and forgo plans for the ice plant. There was more money to be made in mineral water. The Luer brothers considered the proposition and went for it and by 1914 the Mineral Springs Hotel opened on the site that was once meant for the ice facility.

Upon opening, Mineral Springs Hotel became an instant hit with people everywhere. Mineral spring water was bottled and sold like crazy and the hotel's two pools filled with mineral water became a huge attraction. People traveled from all over just to swim in those waters. They claimed that the special spring water contained distinct healing powers that could cure just about anything from aches and pains to hangovers. Some folks even touted the water could cure the common cold, an ailment that still has no cure today. In all likelihood, the water probably never possessed any magical healing properties, but it did contain sulfur so perhaps its strong odor had something to do with the newfound rejuvenation people reported feeling after a quick swig or swim. The buzz over the mineral spring water continued for as long as the Luer brothers operated the hotel. They eventually sold it in 1926 and moved on to other things. The new owners maintained the hotel for a time, but its popularity dwindled as the mineral springs craze died out. Diminished success led to the hotel's demise as it began to lose its original luster. Mineral Springs Hotel was no longer in good condition, and with business almost slowing to a halt, it was finally closed for good in 1971. The building was eventually utilized again, not as a hotel but as a site for assorted shops and other businesses. Although the building may have changed in appearance and function, one thing remains the same—the spirits of Mineral Springs Hotel still haunt the place.

Franklin House & the Lincoln Hotel

Alton's Franklin House has been home to a variety of businesses over the years, and a few ghosts as well. Franklin House was built in 1836 and, at the time, hosted the Alton Marine & Fire Insurance Company and First National Bank & Trust Company. Just a few years later in 1840, the building would be converted to a hotel and operate as such for several years to come. Franklin House Hotel was immensely popular and enjoyed much prosperity, as it provided convenient lodging to travelers along the river. The hotel was even impressive enough to host Abraham Lincoln during the Lincoln-Douglas presidential debates. After Lincoln was elected President two years later, the owners of Franklin House Hotel opted to rename it in his honor, and it probably wasn't bad for business either. The hotel then became known as the Lincoln Hotel. It was also about this time that people began experiencing the first ghostly encounters in the building...many of which continue to this day even in the new businesses that now occupy the former hotel.

One of the most commonly spotted apparitions in the building is that of a young girl dressed in white who prefers to play on the stairs or run through the halls of the old hotel she once called home. Building employees often hear her moving about even when they cannot see her. Sometimes, the faint sound of the little girl's laughter can also be heard gently floating through the air, and there are times when she likes to make contact by brushing against the clothing of those who are near. She has also been known to confiscate personal belongings. She must know better, though, because she always returns them later. So who was this little girl who now haunts the Franklin House?

In the early years of the hotel's operation a traveling salesman secured a room for his family at the Franklin House Hotel. His wife and daughter lived there temporarily while he traveled to various towns along the Mississippi River promoting his products. The man's seven-year-old daughter seemed to be quite happy in the hotel and always managed to entertain herself there. But one day misfortune fell upon the family. While playing outside the girl rushed into the street to retrieve a ball that had gotten away from her. Before anyone could stop it from happening, the little girl was run over and crushed by a heavy wagon as it thundered down the street transporting goods. The child didn't

survive, but her spirit seems to *live on* in the familiar Franklin House building. When the building still functioned as a hotel, guests given the girl's former room often reported feeling icy temperatures in certain areas of the room, as well as hearing unexplained sounds like a child at play. Most of the time, guests didn't remain in the room for long, commonly asking for another room. At times when the room was empty, lights could be seen from outside shining through its windows at night. Maybe the little girl never realized what had happened to her and simply lives on in her last known home. And she might not be alone. Employees of the many businesses that now occupy the building sometimes hear the sound of furniture and other heavy items being moved across the floor, as well as footsteps and dancing coming from an upstairs room that once served as the hotel ballroom. The little girl certainly couldn't make all that racket on her own so it's quite likely that she how has some company.

☠☠☠☠☠

Lewis & Clark Community College

Lewis and Clark Community College is located in the town of Godfrey, near Alton. It began operating in 1971 after taking over the existing campus from a previously all-girls seminary school called Monticello. Following the acquisition of the school, not only was its name changed but new buildings were soon added as well. The biggest change was, of course, the transformation from being an all-girl school to a co-ed one. Despite all the inevitable changes around campus, one thing remained the same, though. The former head mistress, Harriet Haskell, would continue to play an active role on campus. The only problem was she had died in 1907, more than sixty years before the school changed hands and became known as Lewis and Clark Community College.

Monticello College was established in 1838 by Captain Benjamin Godfrey, who also owned the Godfrey, Gilman, & Company warehouse that would later become the site of abolitionist Elijah Lovejoy's murder. Monticello College was run by Harriet Haskell for forty years before she passed away. She ran a tight ship and was protective of her girls. She was so utterly devoted to them and their education that many believe she could not bear to leave the school...even in death. In the years following her death, students reported sometimes seeing Harriet Haskell's spirit walking the hallways of the dorm at night, perhaps still looking after her girls while they slept. Other encounters have included lights turning on and off on their own and an old elevator operating independently at night in the former administration building. Bathroom faucets have also turned on without cause, so that running water is heard in the bathroom even when no one is in there. The hauntings first began after Miss Haskell's death when the school still served Monticello girls. However, the paranormal activity hasn't stopped even though a new school now stands on the grounds. Students continue to report strange sounds, lights turning on and off, and even sightings of a ghostly woman resembling photos of Harriet Haskell. One of her favorite places on campus seems to be the library, which was originally the Monticello chapel as evidenced by its high vaulting ceiling. Librarians have felt the touch of a ghostly hand when working alone after hours, and some have even spotted Harriet Haskell's ghost wearing a dress like what she might have worn to church. When her spirit is present in the library, the scent of lilacs can often be smelled wafting through air as well. It seems neither time nor death can keep Harriet Haskell from maintaining an ever watchful eye over her cherished campus.

Milton School

There's an old school building in the Milton Heights neighborhood of Alton on Milton Road that operated for a full eighty years from 1904 to 1984 before finally closing its doors to students. Although the building no longer functions as a school today, it's still used for other businesses. The first company to occupy space in the former Milton School was Intaglio Design. The home décor company began leasing space in the school in 1990 after the building had been empty for six years. It wasn't long after Intaglio opened that employees began noticing a lot of strange things. For instance, staff would often hear footsteps scuffling across the floor out in the hall while they worked quietly in their offices, yet, when they peeked out for a quick look, no one was ever there. Sometimes employees would leave their offices momentarily only to find various items missing upon their return. Unexplained events happened to many of the employees, but none more so than to one female worker whose office was situated at the bottom of a staircase near the old school gym. Upon returning to her office after having briefly stepped out, this employee would often find random typing on her computer screen, such as "Xs" and "Os" normally signifying hugs and kisses. In most cases this type of activity might be attributed to the office prankster, however, all of her coworkers swore they hadn't done it. This particular employee seemed to be especially prone to all the pranks. It was not unusual for things to go missing from her office or for strange noises to be heard in there, and she frequently observed someone else had been typing at her computer. It was a little unnerving, especially since no one had any idea who could be doing all of those things. If it wasn't a coworker pulling pranks, the only possible explanation was an outsider that had gained access to the building. There had been a few sightings of a young school-aged girl wandering the halls at the bottom of the staircase near the school's old gym. At the time, no one knew who she was, but they would soon discover she was responsible for all the strange activity in the office. What they didn't expect was that she was a ghost!

The ethereal girl was once a student at Milton School when it was still in operation. And, as it turns out, former students of the school used to see her ghostly image in the halls near the old gymnasium long before Intaglia employees ever did. So who was this mysterious student and why does she haunt the school building? Most folks refer to the young spirit as Mary. She seems to be a gentle soul, but the reason she haunts her old school is not a nice one. Mary was a student at Milton sometime during the 1930s. By all accounts she was a diligent student, so much so that it wasn't unusual for her to remain after school to finish assignments. On one particular afternoon, she stayed after to complete a project and would never be seen alive again. After finishing up what she was doing, she likely headed down the empty hallways, shoes scuffling across the floor, until she reached a flight of stairs near the gymnasium. She didn't get much further than that though. In fact, Mary would never exit the building.

When she didn't return home later that evening, her parents' growing anxiety would result in the realization of their worst fears. Mary had met with trouble. Sadly, the young girl's nude body was found in the girl's locker room near the gymnasium where she had last walked. Her clothes were strewn about and it appeared that she had been sexually assaulted. There were many uncertainties as to who could have committed such an unspeakable act and why, but one thing was clear. Mary had fought for her life. Investigators discovered skin fragments and dried blood lodged beneath her fingernails, evidence she had fought back by clawing at her attacker. Unfortunately, DNA testing was not yet a reality and the evidence couldn't be used to identify a potential assailant. At the time, it could only confirm there was as struggle. What could be deduced from the blood and skin evidence, however, was that whoever was guilty of the horrific crime would surely bear the signs of a recent struggle as in scratch marks and surface wounds inflicted by Mary in self-defense.

Within a few days of gathering evidence and questioning everyone who knew Mary, school officials realized that one of the custodial staff could not be accounted for. In fact, he had not been seen since Mary's body was discovered. Investigators quickly located the missing man and observed noticeable scratches on his hands when they were questioning him. A family member provided a firm alibi and the police were left little choice but to let the man go for the time being. Regardless of the man's insistence that he had nothing to do with the crime, rumors spread rapidly and everyone believed him to be guilty. With no one on his side, the man's spirits waned as he became increasingly isolated from the community and the school. But before things could get any worse for the suspected child killer, the man took his own life by hanging himself in the very school where he had been accused of taking Mary's life. Beneath the man's dangling feet was a note that simply read, "I did it." That said it all. The case was closed as far as anyone else was concerned. Unless the man had been simultaneously framed and murdered, it seems likely he was responsible for ending Mary's life. Since her tragic death there have been countless reports of paranormal activity in the building. It's uncertain whether or not the former janitor who took his own life also haunts the building, but the girl he was accused of raping and killing clearly still walks the halls of her old school.

Mayford's Murder

Alton has yet another strange murder case with a ghostly ending—the unsolved murder of Officer August Mayford. Officer Mayford was sixty-six years old and had proudly served with the Alton Police Department for eighteen years. It was just another night on the job when Mayford went missing shortly after a quick dinner with a fellow patrolman at a nearby diner. After both men had finished eating, they headed out into the cool October night around eleven p.m. and went their separate ways, each to patrol his usual beat. Unfortunately, Officer Mayford would never return from his shift.

When Mayford didn't check in after his shift the following morning, fellow officers checked everywhere with no luck. A subsequent investigation didn't turn up many clues either. Two weeks would pass before there was a break in the case. On Halloween, the body of Officer August Mayford was discovered beaten and shot to death in a cornfield near the far edge of a farm on the outskirts of Alton near Edwardsville. Mayford had been shot eight times and his gun was missing so it's possible his own weapon was used against him. Police speculated that Mayford may have interrupted a robbery at one of the stores along his beat. In an attempt to evade capture, the perpetrators likely assaulted and kidnapped Mayford. But since he could identify them, they may have concluded that their only way out was to kill him. And they were right. To this day the case has never been solved. With the absence of any substantial clues, there are no clear suspects and, consequently, no clear-cut motive. One thing is for sure, though: Officer Mayford remains on duty and continues to patrol the streets of downtown Alton with dedication and valor, as witnessed by all those who've seen his spirit still walking the beat.

The Legend of the Great Piasa

This next strange story is steeped in legend and involves not only ghosts, but also a bizarre creature called the Piasa. If you inquire around Alton about the Piasa, you'll likely be directed down the Great River Road to a rocky bluff overlooking the Mississippi River. There you'll find a large mural painted on the side of the cliff. The painting depicts the legendary Piasa creature. The original painting, which was discovered by explorers from Canada in 1673, was eventually destroyed by time, weather, and construction work done at the Alton Penitentiary when Confederate soldiers were confined there. Fortunately, the people of Alton were able to recreate the impressive Piasa painting so that it once again decorates the stone cliffs along the great Mississippi.

So what exactly is this Piasa creature? Today, the odd creature that now adorns the cliffs over the Mississippi River is shown as having large wings, a long tale, a human-like face, a long

beard, horns, and claws with its body completely covered in scales. It appears to be a bizarre dragon-like bird. Interestingly, early descriptions of the creature make no mention of wings so that feature may not be an accurate reflection of the original Piasa. Father Jacques Marquette and Louis Joliet were sent on an expedition seeking a passageway to the Pacific Ocean from Canada. They started off in the waters of chilly Lake Michigan until they eventually wound their way down the Mississippi River to the southern end of Illinois. They never did make it to the Pacific, but they did make a surprising discovery nevertheless when they encountered the strange creature either carved or painted upon the rocky cliffs above as they floated down the river below.

The creature must have left an ominous impression because Father Marquette's description depicted a fearsome creature. In fact, his journal account of the discovery mentions multiple creatures as he continually uses the term "they" when describing the encounter. Perhaps current illustrations have missed the mark and there were at least two fearsome creatures without wings that were more like giant monsters than birds. There are many unanswered questions as to what the original creature really looked like and what it represented. No one even knows who originally carved or painted the Piasa image on the side of the steep cliff. It would have seemed nearly impossible to undertake such a feat all those years ago. To complicate matters even more, various fictitious legends have been concocted over the years offering different accounts of the great Piasa. For instance, in 1836 a professor and writer named John Russell created an elaborate story about the giant man-eating bird that swooped down from above snatching up unsuspecting victims and carrying them off to a secret cave where their bones were discarded after they'd been devoured alive.

Russell's account led to the translation of the name Piasa to mean something like "man devouring bird." Additionally, his story made heroes out of the local Illini tribe when Chief Ouatoga offered himself as bait to the giant bird in order to entrap it so that the chief's men, who were hiding nearby, could take aim and kill the monstrous creature with poisoned arrows. The plan worked and the Piasa was destroyed, never to kill again. Russell's story created quite a buzz when it first appeared in the August issue of *The Family Magazine*, according to researcher and writer John Dunphy. Over the years, the legend of the Piasa has been so strongly associated with Russell's fictitious story involving the Illini tribe that it has come to be accepted as fact, although there is no clear evidence that the Piasa drawing is a Native American creation or that the legend itself stems from tribal tales passed down from one generation to the next.

Other researchers have attempted to link the Piasa to Chinese exploration in the early 1400s, before European explorers would have ever arrived in the Americas. The book, *1421: The Year China Discovered America*, written by Gavin Menzies, offers evidence in support of Chinese explorers happening upon the Americas and other parts of the world in 1421. Another researcher, Mark Nickless, suggests that fantastical creatures of Chinese culture were the inspiration for the original Piasa duo, and perhaps Chinese explorers themselves even carved or painted the creatures on the side of the bluff. There is certainly a great deal of mystery surrounding the legendary Piasa and many questions may continue to go unanswered, but what about ghosts?

The legend of the Piasa is also associated with local ghost lore. It's said that the cave where the mighty Piasa carried its defenseless victims to their grotesque death is haunted by their restless souls. Now, although the Piasa bird itself was likely a fictitious creature, the cave referenced in Russell's story is not. At some point in history, a cave really was discovered hidden deep in the bluffs overlooking the Mississippi River near where the original Piasa picture once loomed. Inside the dark cave were piles of bones—many of which were human. Perhaps the Piasa did stash the remains of its victims in the cave after all, or were these people instead victims of a more foul and sinister fate like that suffered by early visitors of Cave-in-Rock? No one really knows for sure, but you can bet there is something distinctly eerie about a cave with human remains. And if you ever happen upon the legendary Piasa cave, don't be surprised when a shadowy figure or strange sounds creep up on you in the dark.

3

Springfield

Springfield

Springfield is the capital of Illinois and the home of former President Abraham Lincoln. It's located smack in the center of the state and officially became the capital in 1837. The original capital of the state was Kaskaskia, located much further south in the Little Egypt area. It was moved to another town called Vandalia for a time before finally finding its permanent home in present-day Springfield.

Taking a stroll through Springfield is like taking a walk back in time in some ways. There are practically historical buildings on every corner and the legendary Route 66 even runs through there. In fact, Abraham Lincoln's home and the very street on which he once lived have been preserved much as they were in his day. Landmark historic sites like Lincoln's home, the Governor's mansion, Frank Lloyd Wright's Dana House, the Vachel-Lindsay House, and the Inn at 835 all lend a certain charm to Springfield that is unmatched anywhere else. You can easily see all these sites and more during a leisurely stroll through the surprisingly small city. At first glance, Springfield almost looks more like a sleepy little town than the site of a state capital. But dig a little deeper and you'll discover there's much more to this place than meets the eye. In fact, there's quite a lot lurking below the surface...

The Lake Club

One of Springfield's most haunted sites in years past was the Lake Club on Fox Bridge Road. So many different people witnessed the strange paranormal events that occurred there over the years that the club was profiled on an episode of "The Haunting." The show aired on the Discovery Channel in 2005 under the episode title "The Lake Club Horror." What happened at the Lake Club wasn't the usual haunting fare, like strange noises, misplaced items, and cold spots. There seemed to be something more sinister going on.

The Lake Club opened in 1940 under the direction of Harold Henderson and Hugo Giovagnoli who turned the place into a jumping nightclub. It was truly the hotspot in town and catered to Springfield's upper class. The club sported a dance floor, billiards, gambling, big band performances, and other live talent. During the club's successful twenty plus-year run, it saw a score of notable performers, including Bob Hope, Pearl Bailey, Spike Jones, Ella Fitzgerald, Lawrence Welk, Mickey Rooney, and Mel Torme. If you were anywhere near Springfield, the Lake Club was the place to be. That was until it was temporarily shut down following a sting operation resulting in a raid that uncovered illegal gambling and betting taking place in a back room of the club. All sorts of items were confiscated, including a pool table used for craps, several decks of cards, dice, and even the promissory notes of patrons running a gambling tab. It was a big blow to the club, but that didn't necessarily stop it. The club was back up and running before too long but, unfortunately, business was not quite as good as it was before the surprise raid. Business continued to decline until club owners Giovagnoli and Henderson ultimately decided to close the doors on the flailing business in 1968. In addition to the blow of closing the club, another tragic event would occur in association with the club around this same time—one that would later come back to haunt them.

Despite closing for a time, the club would later reopen under the name "The Sober Duck Rock and Disco Club." Giovagnoli and Henderson still owned the space, but they left management of the club to Tom Blasko and Bill Carmean. Giovagnoli remained involved to some extent, coming in to check on things regularly, but Henderson operated more as a silent partner. It was during this time when the club took on a new persona that strange things began happening. At first, just the two managers noticed the strange activity...only neither of them revealed to the other what they had been experiencing. Each thought he was letting his imagination get the best of him. Soon other employees were experiencing unusual events, and in time so too were customers. Paranormal activity included items being tossed on the floor, glasses flying up and smashing against the walls, doors opening and closing, footsteps, restroom hand dryers turning themselves on, piano keys playing, and musicians' instruments going in and out of tune without cause or explanation. But the most unsettling experience occurred when a waitress went to use an employee bathroom in the back of the club and encountered the bizarre apparition of a man's head. From the shape of his face, the man appeared to be heavy set and his hair was white. He issued the startled waitress a foreboding warning. He warned that one of the club owners would die soon. The woman was so disturbed by the encounter that she didn't immediately say anything, but she was extremely worried for both Blasko and Carmean, the current club managers. She couldn't keep the secret for long because they noticed her acting nervously. She finally told them what had happened and they didn't know what to make of it. Needless to say, everyone was feeling more than a little unsettled by it all. What would happen just two weeks later would leave everyone speechless. Harold Henderson, Giovagnoli's silent partner, passed away unexpectedly. The fortune revealed by the sinister apparition had come true.

Things had now gone too far for anyone's taste. Previously, it had all seemed mildly entertaining, but with the death of Henderson—as predicted by the ghostly image—anything could happen from that point on. Blasko then asked a priest friend to come out and investigate. He agreed and brought two other priests with him. The three clergymen came out to the club and determined that there was, in fact, an unhappy spirit haunting the place. They walked through the club room by room and blessed the entire place. They encouraged the lingering spirit to move on and asked that he no longer disturb the Lake Club. From that point on the paranormal activity stopped and it was back to business as usual. In time, though, the club was eventually closed and stood empty for three years before mysteriously burning down in 1992. The circumstances of the fire were questionable, but no arson or insurance fraud charges were ever filed.

So who was the ominous apparition that accurately predicted the death of Lake Club owner Harold Henderson? The female employee to whom the ghost appeared positively identified the face she had seen from a photo Giovagnoli had shown her of former Lake Club employees who worked there in the 1950s and '60s. It turns out that the woman matched the apparition to a photo of an old employee named Albert Cranor who went by the name Rudy. Before the once illustrious Lake Club shut down, Rudy reportedly began experiencing financial difficulties and started drinking excessively on the job. No one knows for sure why, perhaps due to the closing of the club and the implied loss of a job, but Rudy decided to take his own life in a back room of the club in June of 1968 when he shot himself with a rifle. The consensus by all was that Rudy had been responsible for all the unexplained activity in the place, including glasses being thrown at patrons and staff, and the doomsday prediction of Henderson's death. No one really knows why Rudy haunted the place, but when he was gone following the priests' blessing, everyone felt a certain sadness at his departure.

Springfield Theatre Center

The Springfield Theatre Center is a modest building that plays host to the Springfield Theatre Guild whose name appears on the front of the building. The deceptively small exterior of the brick building offers no hint at what lies inside. The movie style auditorium is more than adequate for hosting a full audience before a live stage performance. Beneath the building is a large basement featuring dressing rooms for the actors and storage areas for props. The theatre serves its purpose hosting exceptional plays and musicals, but there's one performer there with his own agenda.

The theatre is said to be haunted by the ghost of one of its former actors, Joe Neville, who performed on the theatre's stage in the 1950s. He was unquestionably talented, yet no one liked him. His grandiose ego prevented him from accruing many friends. Everyone enjoyed his performances, but no one necessarily enjoyed

Springfield Theatre Center sign.

Springfield Theatre Center building.

his personality. It's difficult to understand why a man with such a purportedly massive ego would feel hopeless enough to commit suicide, but that's exactly what Joe did. Following another excellent performance as the lead in one of the theatre's productions, Joe went home and ended his own life.

The only explanation anyone could come up with for why he did such a thing was that he may have taken some theatre funds that didn't belong to him and either feared being caught or was wracked with such guilt he could no longer stand it. Whatever the reason, Joe now roams the theatre he once dominated and he seems to have a penchant for pranks. Joe is known to hide objects or props. He also likes to hide the actors' costumes during the middle of a performance when they need them for quick costume changes. Some actors have even reported being shoved by old Joe. He is known to walk the catwalk and is often identified by the distinct aroma of Noxema, which he had always used for an uncomfortable skin condition. The actors have banned the use of Noxema in the theatre today so when anyone does catch a whiff of the stuff it's clear Joe is somewhere nearby. Who knows if Joe is unhappy with the other actor taking over his stage, but he is certainly just as nasty in death as he was in life.

The Dana Thomas House

The Frank Lloyd Wright Dana House, properly called the Dana Thomas House, was built for Susan Lawrence Dana and designed by the renowned Chicago architect Frank Lloyd Wright. The home that originally stood there was charming enough, but Susan wanted to add on to the small family home. So in 1902 she sought the help of Frank Lloyd Wright. When she first approached him she wanted to add on to the existing Italian villa style house the family already owned. Her plan was to create a space for entertaining guests. When it was all said and done, the house was truly a one-of-a-kind masterpiece. There would be nothing else like it in Springfield at the time. Wright designed the house in an architectural style he called prairie style. It took extensive time and money to complete the house, but Susan felt it was well worth it. The renovations were completed in 1904 and Susan would finally have her dream home. The only thing was...she worried about what her dad might think.

View of the north side of the Dana Thomas House.

Back view of the Dana Thomas House.

View of the Dana Thomas House facing east.

The front entrance of the Dana Thomas House. The house was designed by Frank Lloyd Wright.

Susan couldn't exactly ask her dad if he approved of the home's new look since he had passed away years earlier. In fact, the inheritance he left for her was the reason she was able to renovate anything at all. She made arrangements to conduct a séance with the hope of contacting her father. A spirit medium assisted Susan in successfully contacting him, and she was relieved to find out that he was happy with the work she had done. Unfortunately, Susan's excitement over the new house was cut short when her mother passed away shortly after moving in. As time went on, the house would be all Susan had. She had now lost both parents, and had previously lost a husband and two babies that were never carried to term. With the loss of so many family members, Susan became intrigued by Spiritualism and further dabbled in séances and other related activities. She was known to hold regular séances in her grand home. Over the years the sound of footsteps, voices, and items falling off the walls has convinced many folks the place is haunted, and they attribute it to Susan's strong interest in the other side. Many people believe it is Susan who haunts her old estate.

The Inn at 835

Located just around the corner from Frank Lloyd Wright's Dana House sits the historic landmark Inn at 835 on South Second Street in Springfield's old Aristocracy Hill neighborhood. The Inn offers a charming look at the past in more ways than one. It was built in 1909 and is situated along the original Route 66. It still retains the look and décor of its most prominent years as a premier luxury apartment dwelling for Springfield's elite when it was originally owned by Bell Miller, a successful florist who owned several greenhouses throughout the capital city. For Miss Bell, the Inn wasn't just a house—it was her dream home—and she enjoyed hosting guests there. Over the years, Bell's Inn saw numerous high society tenants and was well known among residents of the city.

Bell Miller was apparently so fond of the home that she has remained there long after her passing. Over the years, staff and visitors alike have reported unexplained happenings. It seems the ghost of Miss Bell is still caring for the home she adored so much. Her spirit seems to be friendly and nurturing and she never causes any problems, although there was a baffling instance in which she repeatedly placed a book in the middle of the floor each time staff of the Inn re-shelved it. Most of the time, Miss Bell seems to be tidying up the place. She even repaired a section of torn wallpaper overnight that had peeled away from the wall the day before. Imagine the staff's surprise when they opened up in the morning! Bell's voice is sometimes heard as she passes through closed doors moving about the house. This is one innkeeper who's always on the job.

The Executive Mansion

View of the Executive Mansion peeking out over the block long brick privacy wall.

Springfield's Executive Mansion has also been called the Governor's Mansion and the Yates Mansion. Abraham Lincoln originally had the idea to construct a home for the state's governor, but the plan would not come to fruition for several decades following Lincoln's assassination. The mansion was built in either 1904 or '05 and was intended to be the home of the Governor of Illinois. The property takes up an entire block and is surrounded on at least two sides by a high brick wall concealing the house from clear view, save for two gates on either side of the house and an iron fence at one end of the property permitting passersby a fleeting glimpse of the grand mansion. The home is just a few blocks walk from the capital building.

As with many of Springfield's historic sites the Executive Mansion is said to be haunted, the origins of which stem from former occupant Richard Yates, Jr. When Yates lived there, his

Secured west entrance to the Executive Mansion.

View of the front of the Executive Mansion from the landscaped yard.

Attic window looking out from the Romance Room in the Executive Mansion.

Springfield's capitol building.

favorite place in the entire house was a stuffy little attic room high up in the house with a round window overlooking the property. Yates was known to spend hours in the small room reading and reflecting on things. Although it is unclear why based on the dismal unfinished appearance of the room, Yates often referred to it as the Romance Room. He was so attached to the room that he has remained there ever since. From the master bedroom below, his ghost can regularly be heard pacing the worn wood floors of the dusty upper attic room on nights when there's a full moon.

The Lincoln Home

The Lincoln Home.

The ghosts of both Abraham and Mary Lincoln are reported to haunt their Springfield home at 413 South Eighth Street. The house has long been purported to be haunted, especially by Lincoln's wife and maybe even their young son who died when he was only eleven. Mary Lincoln's spectral form can sometimes be seen walking about the house from room-to-room. Additionally, children's toys have been observed moving around as though a child were playing with them.

Workers in the home have noticed other strange occurrences on several occasions. Items are sometimes moved around to different locations in the house and furniture is even discovered in another room altogether from where it was originally. Candles have been discovered burnt down in the morning as if they'd been burning all night. And some staff members, and even guests, have reported feeling a hand tap them when no one is around. Voices can also be

Side view of the Lincoln Home.

View of the Lincoln home from the south side of the home.

One of the historic homes on Lincoln's block.

Lincoln's block has many historic homes...like this one.

View looking north up South Eight Street directly in front of the Lincoln Home.

heard, as can the swishing of Mrs. Lincoln's dress as she passes by down the hall. A few lucky individuals have actually caught a quick glimpse of Mrs. Lincoln's spectral image.

Lincoln's ghost sometimes makes an appearance as well. It's not unusual for his rocking chair to independently begin swaying steadily back and forth as though he was still sitting there contemplating the fate of our great nation. The Lincolns acquired the home in 1844 when it was just five-years-old. Today the National Park Service has restored the home, as well as most of the neighborhood, to its original appearance during the time when Lincoln resided there. With their home intact much as it was when they lived there, it's no wonder the Lincolns feel comfortable there now all these years later.

President Lincoln

No discussion of Springfield's history, haunted or not, would be complete without mentioning President Abraham Lincoln who is the city's most notable ghost. Lincoln's ghost has been spotted all around Springfield, including his home, his old law offices, the courthouse, and the site of his tomb in Oak Ridge Cemetery. Poet Nicholas Vachel Lindsay, husband of Lincoln's wife Mary Todd's sister, composed a poem about the presidential apparition. The most famous lines read as follows:

"It is portentous, and a thing of state; that here at midnight in our little town; a mourning figure walks, and will not rest; near the old courthouse pacing up and down."

What is interesting about Vachel Lindsay's words is the connotation that Lincoln's ghost was mournful. If so, was he mourning his own passing? Or could it have been the tragic loss of his son Willie to illness at age eleven? Perhaps it was even the death of his first love, Ann Rutledge, who he'd been involved with in New Salem before ever meeting his wife. In life Lincoln seemed to carry the weight of the world on his shoulders as he bore the responsibility of leading the nation quite seriously. Maybe his somber demeanor in death is merely a reflection of that, yet a look back at Lincoln's life reveals some fatalistic tendencies.

Lincoln had two strange experiences that possibly foretold the tragedy of his assassination by John Wilkes Booth in the Ford's Theater in 1865. The first experience was a vision Lincoln had in which he saw his face reflected twice in the mirror. One of the images of is face appeared somewhat paler in color than the other. He had this vision more than once and, when he discussed it with his wife, she suggested that the two faces signified he'd be elected to two presidential terms, which was certainly good news. Unfortunately, she believed that one of the faces appearing to be so extremely pale was a dark sign that Lincoln would not live out his full second term, but would instead die before it was over.

Another interesting experience of Lincoln's was a dream that would later seem to have been a premonition of his own death. Lincoln

Vachel Lindsay House where Nicholas Vachel Lindsay wrote about Lincoln's ghost.

reported having a dream in which he awoke in his upstairs bedroom in the White House and heard people crying downstairs. He got up and walked out of his room, down the hall, and down the stairs. He continued to hear the sad sobbing, but saw no one. He made his way to the East Room of the White House and observed a large gathering of people all mourning a death. There was a body wrapped up in funeral garb. The face was completely covered and guards stood all around. When he asked who was laying there dead in the White House, a guard replied that it was the president and that he had been killed by an assassin. According to close confidants of Lincoln's, he did not believe the dream told of his own assassination, but of someone else's. He insisted his friends were all wrong when they worried for his life. He seemed to think it nonsense that anyone would be trying to kill him and joked that they should quit trying to protect him from some unknown stranger who might be plotting to kill him. Ironically, President Lincoln was assassinated not long after that prophetic dream.

Many people claim that prior to his death, Lincoln was involved with a group called the Spiritualists and was extremely interested in astrology, prophecy, ghost lore, and the like. Lincoln experts insist this isn't true. They claim the Spiritualists attempted to associate themselves

Side view of the Vachel Lindsay House.

with Lincoln after his assassination in order to gain notoriety for themselves and their beliefs. Lincoln historians suggest that it was Lincoln's wife who was actually curious about the Spiritualists, and had developed an interest following the death of their eleven-year-old son Willie. It seems Mrs. Lincoln hosted several séances at the White House, which gave rise to the claims that Lincoln himself was a Spiritualist. There is even speculation that during one particular séance, the piano levitated right off the floor. Despite Mary Todd Lincoln's fascination with the Spiritualists, there is no clear evidence to suggest that Lincoln was also heavily involved with them.

What the evidence does show in countless documented sightings is that Lincoln's ghost does persist and isn't bound to a single location.

There are conflicting perspectives on whether or not his spirit haunts his old home, but there are numerous corroborating accounts of his ghost seen wandering near the Lincoln Tomb Monument. Additionally, Lincoln's ghost is believed to also haunt the White House in Washington D.C. Former President Theodore Roosevelt was a firm believer in the presence of Lincoln's ghost in the White House and claimed to have seen him in various rooms and hallways within the building. Former First Lady Grace Coolidge was the first person to ever report seeing Lincoln's ghost there when she observed him looking out a window in the Oval Office while her husband Calvin Coolidge was President.

Other notable individuals to have witnessed Lincoln's ghost in the White House include Queen Wilhelmina of the Netherlands and President Ronald Reagan's daughter Maureen. During Queen Wilhelmina's visit with the Roosevelts, she was awakened in the middle of the night by a knock at her bedroom door. When she opened it, she was surprised to see the image of Abraham Lincoln standing there before her. Reagan's daughter Maureen and her husband both reported seeing the ghost of Lincoln in the White House as well. With all the sightings of Lincoln around Springfield and D.C., it seems he's just as busy now as he was in life. Perhaps he'll finally rest some day, but for now he continues to roam all the places to which he was so closely linked in life.

Lincoln's Tomb

The receiving vault at Oak Ridge Cemetery where Lincoln's body was originally brought prior to burial.

Two views of the Lincoln Tomb & Monument: one shows the beautiful landscape surrounding the Monument, the other, the former President's likeness.

The Lincoln statue atop his monument.

Lincoln's grand tomb stands tall on a hill in Oak Ridge Cemetery, but it wasn't always his final resting place. The tomb was dedicated in 1860—five full years after Lincoln's death.

Rather than bury Lincoln near the White House where he lived and worked at the time of his assassination, friends and family requested he be buried in Springfield, the city he loved so dearly. His body was transported from Washington D.C. to Springfield by train. Rather than take a straight line there, the train was routed in such a way as to pass by as many onlookers between the two cities as possible. As the train passed through one

Original caretaker's home just a few yards away from the Lincoln Tomb at Oak Ridge Cemetery.

city after another, mourners lined up to see the coffin bearing the honorable President as it sat securely atop a flatcar on the train. In total, the train traveled close to 1,700 miles before reaching its final destination and Lincoln's final resting place. Even today it's still possible to catch a glimpse of the funeral procession and you don't have to go to a museum to do so. Sometimes the spectral image of the train that carried Lincoln's body on that long somber journey in 1865 can still be seen slowly chugging along the tracks making its way to Springfield. In most sightings, there is usually a lead train in which all the cars are draped in black that forges the way. It's often heard playing a funeral dirge as it passes followed by a second train pulling only a single flatcar bearing Lincoln's coffin.

Don't worry if you miss out on witnessing the phantom funeral procession because you can catch a glimpse of Honest Abe himself at the site of his tomb. However, Lincoln's present day tomb wasn't completed until five years after his death. Prior to that, he had been buried in a temporary tomb after being released from the receiving vault. Incidentally, the cemetery's

Governor's tomb across from the Lincoln Tomb & Monument at Oak Ridge Cemetery.

original receiving vault is located just on the other side of the hill on which his tomb, and final resting place, now stands. The body of Lincoln's son Willie, who had died three years earlier, was also brought to Oak Ridge Cemetery to be buried with his father. In time, the entire family would be buried there except for his son Robert, who was buried in Arlington National Cemetery. Lincoln's body was reportedly moved several times during the five-year period that his tomb was being constructed to prevent vandals or grave robbers from causing problems. Apparently, there were several plots to steal the President's body. When the tomb was finally completed, it featured a marble interior, portions of which were obtained from France, Italy, Belgium, and Spain, as well as from the states of Utah, Arkansas, Minnesota, Massachusetts, and Missouri. With materials being brought in from all corners of the earth, it's no wonder it took so long to construct. Some folks believe that all the commotion in moving Lincoln's body around prior to the completion of the tomb may

Isolated staircase near the receiving vault at Oak Ridge Cemetery.

have caused him a bit of unrest. It's been said that Lincoln's ghost can be seen wandering near the tomb on occasion, as can the ghost of a little boy who just might be his beloved son Willie. Other witnesses have reported hearing phantom voices and footsteps in and around the tomb. For many, there's no question Lincoln walks the cemetery grounds, but whether his body is actually laid to rest in the monument tomb or is hidden away somewhere secret is another question!

New Salem

Lincoln and Ann Rutledge

New Salem sits in a beautiful location overlooking the Sangamon River, but no one actually lives there. The small settlement, as it appears today, is actually a reconstruction of the original village. Its rustic log cabins and quaint businesses have been preserved as the Lincoln's New Salem State Historic Site. New Salem served as Lincoln's home for six years prior to his relocation to Springfield where he would practice law and become involved in politics and government. Many people credit Lincoln with founding New Salem, but it was already established when he traveled up the river from St. Louis in a vessel that wasn't fit to float. Lincoln was steering a flatboat along the Sangamon River when the boat got stuck and developed a hole. A very young Lincoln ordered the crew to begin tossing things overboard as he swam ashore to retrieve items to repair the hole. He did so successfully and continued on, but returned later to stay.

Lincoln enjoyed life in New Salem and even met a girl. Ann Rutledge was betrothed to another man, but when that man traveled out of state and did not return, Lincoln began courting Ann. They fell madly in love and things were wonderful until Ann's former fiancé returned to town. He claimed to have been delayed because his father and two brothers had unexpectedly passed away while he was visiting. Additionally, Ann's fiancé had fallen seriously ill while away and was unable to get back to New Salem or send word of his plight. With the return of her former flame, Ann felt obligated to still marry him though her heart was with Lincoln. It was a devastating turn of events for Ann and the young Abraham Lincoln. But things took a turn for the worse once more, as Ann fell gravely ill. The last time Lincoln would see her, Ann's family recalled watching him walk quietly out of the house and collapse beneath the cool shade of a large tree before breaking down into tears. Ann would die that summer in 1835. Even though Lincoln would later meet and marry Mary Todd, some people believed he never truly got over Ann Rutledge, as she had been his one true love. Those who knew him best suggested that he took on a more solemn demeanor following Ann's untimely death—one that he would carry with him until his own death in 1865. Lincoln relocated to Springfield to practice law after Ann's passing. There, along with his new career, he could also start a new life.

And the Other Ghosts...

There have been two distinct apparitions spotted in the reconstructed New Salem. Interestingly, neither is believed to be Ann Rutledge who died there. Some say good old Abe sometimes walks through New Salem, but it's more likely he sticks mainly to Springfield. Of the two ghosts that do dwell in New Salem, one is a man and the other a woman. The male apparition is most often spotted near the Kelso-Miller cabin and is believed to be the spirit of Jack Kelso. The Kelso-Miller cabin is actually two cabins joined together, which Jack Kelso had dwelled in along with his brother-in-law and their wives. Jack Kelso always loved living in New Salem, which might explain why he's returned, but he didn't die there. He actually moved to Missouri with his brother-in-law when New Salem began to decline as river traffic halted due to a severe drop in the water level of the Sangamon River. Kelso had been disappointed when the family relocated to Missouri, so perhaps he has returned to New Salem to finish living the life he once loved so much.

New Salem's female ghost is believed to be that of a woman named Elizabeth Herndon who was accidentally shot by her husband while he was loading a shot gun in preparation to go hunting. Her death was witnessed by Ann Rutledge's ten-year-old sister Nancy, who had been sent by Lincoln to borrow some tools from Mr. Herndon. Nancy sat and chatted with Mrs. Herndon while she waited for Mr. Herndon to finish what he was doing. While he was fiddling with the gun, it accidentally fired and shot his wife in the neck right before young Nancy's eyes. Mrs. Herndon's death was ruled an accident, but some folks aren't so sure. So while Kelso's ghost seems to haunt New Salem out of his love for the place, Mrs. Herndon's might haunt for her untimely death. Both apparitions have been spotted near their respective former homes and almost immediately vanish into thin air whenever anyone approaches too closely. Sometimes they aren't even seen at all, but their presence is felt. It's as though they are silently watching you from a distance.

4

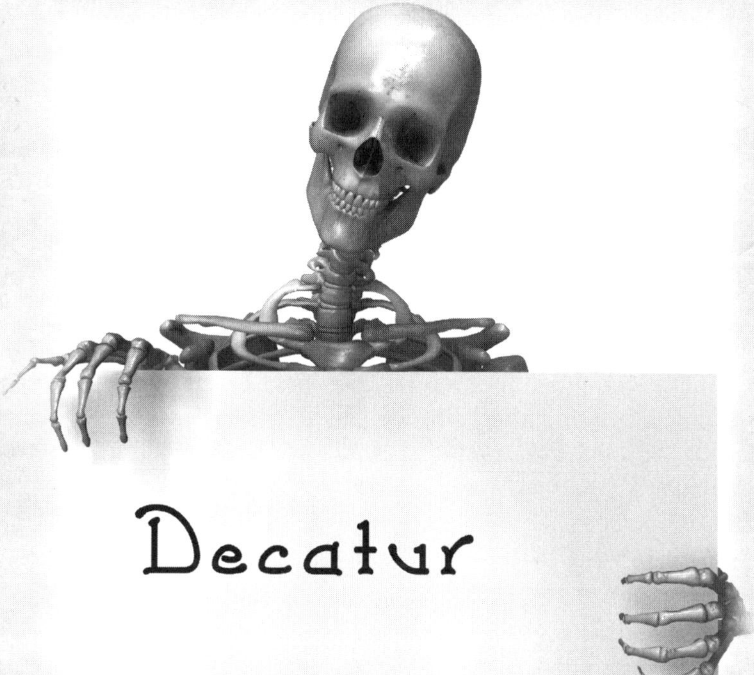

Decatur

Decatur

The city of Decatur is less than an hour's drive from Springfield and was named in honor of Naval Commodore Stephen Decatur who fought at Tripoli and in the War of 1812. Decatur was officially recognized as a county in 1845, although just three hundred people lived there then. As the town continued to grow, so did hostilities between the north and the south in the rest of the country. In the midst of the divide between abolitionist states and those still supporting slavery, several stations on the Underground Railroad began popping up all around Decatur—and many are now part of some of Decatur's most haunted locations. In time, slavery ended and the Civil War passed. It was time for a new era in Decatur. The population grew, business boomed, and railroad transportation came to town. Times were good.

The city continued to flourish and eventually even formed a football team called the Decatur Staleys that would someday relocate and become better known as the Chicago Bears. Decatur's got a great history, and in recent years, it's become known especially for its hauntings thanks to resident ghost expert Troy Taylor.

The Lincoln Theater

The Lincoln Theater was once a grand showplace and the pride of Decatur. It was of such repute that it even boasted a performance by the one and only Harry Houdini early in his career. Today the Lincoln Theater only opens on occasion for special functions, but it isn't necessarily empty—it's home to several occupants of a ghostly nature. Over the years, the Lincoln Theater has come to be known as one of the most haunted places in all of Decatur. *Untraceable footsteps*, *shadowy figures*, *disembodied voices*, *noises*, and *frigid chills in the air*...they are all common occurrences at the Lincoln.

One of the Lincoln's most beloved ghosts is that of a man nicknamed "Red" for his fiery red hair. Red's haunting of the theater began after a freak accident cost him his life. Red was a stagehand who worked behind the scenes to ensure that the various productions put on there always went smoothly, but during a performance one evening, something went tragically wrong. As Red worked some props from high above the stage—up on the catwalk—his arm was caught in one of the pulley mechanisms and he was pulled over the catwalk. Unfortunately, the pulley could not hold him and he plunged to the stage below. The worst of it was that his arm had been caught in the pulley and was actually torn off as his grip slowly slipped until he finally fell. As Red lay lifeless upon the stage before an entire audience, his severed limb was still hanging high above. What a truly gruesome way to go! Fortunately for Red, that account might not be completely true.

While Red was a stagehand at the Lincoln Theater for several years, some reports indicate that he may have actually lost his arm while fighting in World War I. He took the job as stagehand at the Lincoln upon returning home from the war after he had already lost his arm. The real story of his death, according to some folks, is that he passed away in his sleep while napping on a lunch break. Whichever account of his passing is true, it's generally agreed that he loved the theater enough to have wanted to remain for eternity, and so his benevolent spirit continues to climb the catwalk after all these years.

In addition to the presence of Red's ghost, there are other spirits roaming the theater as well.

☠ **Dark shadowy figures are sometimes spotted in the back corner of the stage near a spiraling metal staircase on which phantom footsteps can occasionally be heard clanging against the cold metal.**

☠ **A female apparition is known to sit in the balcony before a performance on stage as though she wants to be the first one in the audience.**

☠ **Other spirits seem to enjoy the shows as well. Entire rows of folding seats have been seen pushed down in the seated position as if occupied...and those same seats are also observed to lift up again just about the time the phantom guests have stood up ready to depart.**

Some of these other ghosts have not been identified, as Red has, but it's possible they are former guests of a hotel that once stood on the site before the theater was ever built. The hotel was ravaged by fire in 1904 and rebuilt, but it burnt down again in 1915 when a boiler room fire blazed out of control. At least two individuals were confirmed to have died in the blaze this time. Several other hotel guests could not be located after the building burned down and may have also perished in the fire. Rather than build another hotel, the lot sat empty until the Lincoln Theater was eventually constructed in 1916. The spirits of those who perished in the hotel fire the year before may have been attached to the grounds on which the hotel once stood and were already there when the Lincoln was built.

The Avon Theater

The first actual movie theater in Decatur was the Avon. Its long history began with its inception in 1916. The arrival of the Avon Theater and the introduction of movies on the big screen generated lots of excitement. The theater had a successful run for a while, but eventually closed down as other theaters cropped up in the area. The building sat empty for an extended period of time and began to deteriorate so much that it was close to being demolished at one point. Fortunately, the timeless theater persists...as do the gregarious spirits that reside there.

Those closest to the theater insist it is home to countless ghosts who enjoy playfully teasing patrons to let them know they're not alone. People who are most familiar with the Avon insist the spirits mean no harm. In fact, they enjoy their presence and would never wish them away.

One of the ghosts has been identified as Gust Constan, a former owner and operator of the Avon. Constan and his brothers ran the theater for over forty years. Following Gust's death in 1965, his brothers opted to lease the theater to another company rather than continue operating it themselves. Many believe that Gust loved the Avon to such an extent that he would have elected to remain there...even in death. And he probably wasn't too pleased with the idea of new management taking over after his brothers leased the theater out, so he may have chosen to stick around and keep an eye on things.

An especially haunted area of the theater is an upstairs hallway where a few offices are located. Gust used to work in an office up there and it's believed that his spirit is most active in that area of the theater, but he isn't the only ghost in town. There are many other spirits roaming the theater, but that particular hallway has quite possibly been the scene of more paranormal activity than anywhere else in the entire building. Not only are cold spots and uncanny feelings of being watched or followed common up there, but many people have come face-to-face with numerous ghostly figures.

In other areas of the theater, ghosts have been spotted sitting and watching the screen as if attending a movie screening. Footsteps, laughter, applause, and voices have also been heard emanating from the empty theater as though it had a full crowd for the night. Other frequent paranormal activity has included items mysteriously going missing. Several theatergoers have even reported being touched by the fun-loving ghosts, sometimes feeling their hair ruffled by spectral hands.

Ghost investigator and author Troy Taylor has had several experiences of his own at the Avon. He's even reported seeing a ghost in the upstairs hallway above the lobby and felt his shirt being pulled in that same hallway. His experiences are not out of the ordinary, as others have had similar encounters with the unknown. According to Troy Taylor, an associate of his has also seen a ghost while working in one of the offices located in that same hallway. Perhaps they both had a run-in with the ghost of good old Gust Constan. But Gust isn't confined to the office area only. Troy Taylor reports that during a haunted tour of the theater, at the very moment the person leading the tour spoke the name of Gust Constan, the man's spirit appeared on an upper balcony in front of the entire tour group. Needless to say, everyone was taken aback, but they sure got their money's worth.

☠☠☠☠☠

Gambling, Ghosts, & Murder at the Speakeasy

During the Prohibition era in our country, it was illegal to make and sell beer, wine, whiskey, and other alcoholic beverages. That didn't stop people from wanting a drink, though. Alcohol may have been outlawed, but bootlegging ran rampant. A number of businesses and homes established secret rooms where people could come for a drink without risk of arrest. Downtown Decatur had its own speakeasy located on Merchant Street in an upstairs floor of an existing business. There, people could drink and gamble in peace. Two adjoining rooms on the third floor served as the speakeasy. When alcohol was no longer banned, the speakeasy continued to operate, mainly promoting gambling and prostitution. Business eventually waned with the onset of the Great Depression. Once the speakeasy operation closed for good, the two rooms were never used again. To this day, they stand virtually empty, save for a few vintage pin-up reminders of yesteryear still adorning the old faded walls.

Haunting activity was first noticed in the speakeasy sometime during the 1990s when renovations began on many of the old historic buildings along the streets of downtown Decatur. Various workers and employees of the different shops and businesses occupying the building then and now have reported hearing voices, period music, and even the sound of a spinning roulette wheel from the closed off rooms of the former speakeasy. Behind the locked doors, it often sounded as though a party was carrying on. Phantom footsteps have also been heard overhead pacing the upstairs floors when no one is actually up there.

The few times anyone was brave enough to venture up to the third floor inside the old speakeasy, the two rooms always felt extremely cold even in the midst of summer, and there was no air conditioning. Strange lights have also been observed in the room. And besides the speakeasy, paranormal activity has occurred throughout the building including unusual sounds and missing items. In fact, a jewelry store on site had several strange instances of the jewelry display cases being unlocked and opened during the night, yet nothing was ever stolen and the alarm system was never triggered. It was as though someone simply wanted to admire the beautiful pieces up close. Even more interesting was an incident involving a missing bottle of whiskey that seemed to indicate the spirits of the speakeasy's former patrons still had a thirst for the forbidden liquor of days gone by.

Harrold House

Moving into a beautiful new house, one you've always dreamed of, can be quite an exciting experience. Imagine how differently you'd feel after finally getting settled in your new home...only to discover you *weren't* living there alone. Instead, you had the feeling that someone was always watching you. That's exactly what happened to several different occupants of the Harrold House on West Wood Street in Decatur over the years.

Anytime a new family moved in they soon had the feeling of being watched. Sometimes they even felt as though they were being followed throughout the house. In time, it would become clear that *three* separate ghosts lived in the house right alongside the current owners. The first ghost sighting occurred when an older male apparition appeared in the upstairs window of the master bedroom. He would be seen there again many times—and by many different witnesses—over the years. Originally, he was only spotted in the room at night looking out the window facing the street as if watching for visitors or people passing by. In time, he began to be observed during daylight hours as well and wasn't always looking through the window at people outside. Instead, he began watching people *inside* the house...seemingly watching anyone entering the master bedroom. This strange specter seemed to be aware of the "living" occupants of the house. The identity of this peering apparition has given rise to the home being dubbed the Harrold House, named for a previous owner who is believed to haunt the house.

From 1922 to 1951, a man named Frank Harrold lived in the house. Harrold worked for a bank and was fairly well off, at least for a while. In 1925, he began experiencing extensive financial difficulties. Something suspicious must have been going on at his place of employment because bank officials began conducting audits. What they discovered was that more than $200,000 in bonds was missing. Although not immediately accused of anything, Harrold must have been worried because he began acting rather peculiarly. He decided to take a few days off to visit his second home in the nearby town of Clinton. He left and was never heard from again. It was starting to look like he had stolen the money and made a run for it. Unfortunately for the bank that money would never be recovered, but the body of Frank Harrold was. He was found at his Clinton estate by one of the hired hands. Frank had been shot in the head, the bullet still lodged inside. Circumstances suggested murder, but investigators would have everyone believe he'd committed suicide. It is significant to note that Harrold had not left any type of suicide note, as is generally common. Likewise, the gun used to kill him wasn't even found anywhere near his cold corpse, but in another location altogether. It just didn't seem feasible that he could have fatally shot himself in the head and then dumped the gun several yards away nor does it seem likely that he stumbled forward several yards after shooting himself since there was no blood trail from the murder weapon to his body. So if Frank Harrold didn't kill himself, then who did?

That mystery would never be solved, just as the money would never be recovered. The scandal of the missing money tarnished the bank's name and reputation enough to force it to close its doors. But it seems Harrold's widow might have known a thing or two about the missing funds. She lived quite well following his death despite not having been granted any of the funds from his life insurance policy since his death was ruled a suicide. Additionally, the Harrolds had been financially strapped just prior to the scandal and his subsequent murder. Mrs. Harrold didn't work and never remarried, so how did she manage to support herself so comfortably for all those years? Could her husband have really been guilty of stealing the missing bank bonds and left them for her? We'll probably never know the answer to that—not unless the ghost of Frank Harrold finally does more than just make spectral appearances to the current occupants of the house anyway. Perhaps one day he'll find a way to leave a message both about who killed him and about the whereabouts of the missing money.

In the meantime, Frank continues to haunt the house and has a few accomplices to boot. The ghosts of both a young boy and a woman have been seen in the house on occasion. The boy is described as having blond hair and is typically dressed in vintage clothing. He's most often observed playing in the old parlor room that sits in the back of the house. The ghost of a young woman, also in vintage period clothing, has been seen standing out on the front porch of the house. The little boy and the woman both only appear sporadically, and may or may not be aware of the living occupants of the house as they never seem to acknowledge anyone as Frank Harrold's ghost does. Unlike Frank, who's ghostly image has been matched to actual pictures of him by present and past owners of the house, there are few clues as to the identity of these other two ghosts. One of the only hints we have comes from a recent owner of the Harrold House who one day heard the boy ghost whisper for his Aunt Francis. As it turns out, one of Frank Harrold's daughters was named Francis. The boy may very well have been Frank's grandchild, and the young woman either Frank's daughter Francis or her sister who would be the young child's mother. But you never know. It might even be the spirit of Frank's wife still enjoying the charming home and comfortable life he left behind for her.

Powers Mansion

The landmark Powers Mansion on West Decatur Street was once owned by the impressive Powers family who had made a name for themselves upon first arriving in the city in 1839. Back then, one look at the house and its robust pillars was a clear indication that the Powers family was doing well for themselves. These days the historic grand mansion is known more for a mean-spirited female apparition who enjoys antagonizing men.

The first Powers family members to arrive in Decatur were brothers George and Samuel Powers. The two brothers enjoyed much success in their newfound home, but it would be the son of their older brother Orlando who would leave behind the legacy of the legendary Powers Mansion. When he was only sixteen, Orlando Powers set sail for Havana, Cuba from New York. He was on his way to visit a fourth Powers brother named William. Orlando never made it across the rough ocean waters, though. The ship he was on went down and he drifted along with some of the debris from the wreck for a full eleven days. Luckily, he was rescued by some sailors who brought him back to France with them. He had nothing to his name, but was able to secure enough funds with the help of some new friends to make his way back to America. Upon arriving home, his family must have first thought him a ghost, as they had not realized he'd survived the shipwreck. Orlando didn't stay in New York long and eventually set out for Illinois to meet his two younger brothers in Decatur. Sadly, his brother George had died just three weeks shy of Orlando's arrival there.

Orlando had a son named Charles, who would go on to own the now famous Powers Mansion on West Decatur Street. The house was built in 1910 and he was only able to enjoy it for two and a half decades before he passed away in 1926. The house did remain in the Powers family for a few more years after Charles' death before his son Jack finally sold it. The once grand home was abandoned around 1961 and began to deteriorate until it was later refurbished and converted to apartments. Serving as a rental property didn't last long, though, as it was again abandoned at some point and began falling apart. Its dilapidated condition grew so extreme that it was practically beyond repair and was set to be torn down until the Bachrach Company purchased and restored it. The extensive renovations that were undertaken on the property apparently awakened some long dormant spirits because strange things started happening around the home. But even before restoration efforts had begun, there were early reports of ghostly figures peeking out through the upstairs windows and strange orbs of light floating about during the extended period of abandonment. On other occasions security motion detectors have gone off when the house was completely empty. The most alarming activity is the maltreatment of male guests, who have reported personal belongings mysteriously vanishing without a trace, as well as aggressive physical assaults on them. Some have even been woken up during the night to their beds being violently shaken. The only possible explanation to account for why male visitors are so antagonistically stalked and targeted is a tragedy that occurred in the house when it functioned as an apartment building. Allegedly a woman was severely beaten and killed by her boyfriend there. Some say the murdered woman now stalks the halls of the house taking revenge on any and all men she encounters for the cruel fate she suffered at the hands of her own beau.

☠☠☠☠☠

The Race Mansion

The Race Mansion used to stand on North Water Street before being torn down in 1915. It was owned by Judge John Race, who wasn't actually a judge of any sort, but had acquired the nickname after judging several events at the Macon County Fair one year. In 1870, Judge Race purchased an empty plot of land that was occupied only by a small private family cemetery at the time. Without disturbing the graves, the judge had a gorgeous Italian villa style house constructed on the land complete with an upper balcony sometimes referred to as a "widow's walk." Reportedly, this widow's walk would become one of the judge's favorite places to relax, as he was able to see all across the sprawling town of Decatur. Judge Race and his family lived in the stunning home for nearly forty years until his wife passed away in 1908 and he followed in 1910. Both Race and his wife were buried in nearby Greenwood Cemetery, a place with its own hauntings where restless spirits walk the grounds at night.

The Race House remained uninhabited for several years after the judge's death, but many Decatur citizens didn't necessarily believe it to be empty. The ghost of Judge Race was sometimes spotted either up on the widow's walk or looking out over the city from an upstairs window. His ghost continued to make occasional appearances around the house for the next five years before the building was torn down to make way for new construction in the developing downtown area. But just because the old Race Mansion was demolished doesn't mean the judge's spirit has left the place. Near the site of the original mansion now stands the Avon Twins, two theater screens associated with the infamous Avon Theater directly across the street. Unusual happenings are said to occur at the twins, particularly when Judge Race's name is spoken aloud. In fact, during a tour at the twin theaters, the group viewing the place was startled when they all simultaneously felt a significant drop in temperature just as their guide uttered the name "Judge John Race" during the course of a story about the old Race Mansion that had previously stood there. When the judge's name was said aloud, it was as though he were suddenly right there with them. And on another occasion, not only did an arctic chill slice through the air like a knife, but all of the lights flickered out as well. Who knows what the spirit of Judge Race is doing these days without his former home, but at least he can occupy himself with an occasional movie.

The Culver House

The Culver House is another of Decatur's landmark mansions. It sits along Prairie Street in the historical district of Decatur. And like both the Race and Powers Mansions, the Culver House is home to several spirits. The house was once a beautiful site, but is now aging and in poor condition. Some folks believe the land on which the house was built to have possibly been cursed. One explanation is that when it was being constructed workers discovered bones and skulls. Clearly the place previously served as a burial ground, possibly used by tribes of the Illiniwek Indian Nation, or perhaps a private family. There was something about that land, though. Before it would come to be known as the Culver House, a man named Josiah Clokey purchased it and began construction on the large home in 1881, but he never finished. Without explanation, Clokey simply abandoned the project before construction was complete. Perhaps paranormal events scared him off. The house sat empty and unfinished for nearly twenty years before John Culver finally purchased the property in 1901. Culver was quite industrious and, in addition to finishing the house, he was reportedly credited with bringing heat and electricity to the downtown Decatur area. He also owned a grave monument business and worked on the Lincoln Tomb and Monument in the nearby city of Springfield.

Culver lived in the house throughout his adult life, and, following his death in 1943, people passing by often observed his image peeking out through the windows, especially from the library. Apparently, Culver wasn't ready to leave his beloved home, not even in death. He doesn't haunt alone, though. Since his passing, he's been joined by the spirits of tenants who lived in the house years after Culver and his family first did when it was later converted into an apartment building. Many of these spirits are the sad souls of former tenants who died in the building. With countless renters over the years, the building saw its share of both good times and tragedy, including a suicide and even a murder. For instance, years ago a young woman took her own life in an upstairs apartment and another woman was killed by her boyfriend in their apartment around 1988. Not long after both the suicide and the murder, the entire building was determined uninhabitable and everyone living there was left with no choice but to find other housing. They might not have minded, though, considering all the negative energy that had accumulated there and the haunting activity. Culver House continues to sit empty today, save for the ghosts still locked inside.

Danzeisen Meat Packing Plant

Decatur's Danzeisen Meat Packing Plant was originally built and owned by G. J. Danzeisen and his partner Adam Blenz back in 1871. The plant was constructed along South Main Street near one of Decatur's two railways and directly across from Greenwood Cemetery, another haunted hot spot in Decatur. The plant operated successfully for a number of years, but would eventually become associated with more than just meat. At some point, plant employees working the night shift began to feel more than a little unsettled by some strange things that were going on *after* hours. The most disturbing phenomenon was the loud sound of the heavy freight elevator traveling up and down from one floor to another. Night workers even heard the elevator gate lift up and close repeatedly as though someone were getting on and off, but each time they checked the elevator to see who was messing around, there was never anyone there. So who was operating the elevator late into the night? As plant workers soon realized, somebody was riding that elevator. They just happened to be a ghost.

Who are these lingering spirits and where did they come from? There's an interesting story about that. Two cattle ranch hands delivering cattle to the meat packing plant arrived late one evening and elected to stay the night in the plant with the cattle. It was as good a place as any, and it was free. Whether or not the men had a restful sleep is anybody's guess, although there is reason to believe they slept quite soundly. So soundly, in fact, that they may have failed to wake up at a critical moment when their lives were in danger. When plant workers arrived early the next morning, they were pleased to see all the cattle had arrived safely. The two ranchers, however, were nowhere to be found—and were never heard from again. The men had seemingly disappeared. Now why would they leave without getting paid? That made no sense. Something must have happened to them, but what?

It's possible the men were really there all along. They may just have been unrecognizable. Legend has it that the sleeping men were tossed in with other "meats" and ground into sausage! Did some malicious worker do this on purpose or was it simply a terrible accident? That's the golden question. Had the men been light sleepers, they might have awakened in time to save themselves. It seems they got their revenge, though. The elevator hauntings certainly scared the pants off the plant workers from the day of their disappearance to the day that the plant eventually closed. Even though the old brick building of the packing plant remains and now houses another company, no one has reported any further paranormal activity. The spirits of the sausage-packed ranchers seem to have been satisfied with the closing of the plant, or maybe they followed their enemies to wherever they went after closing the meat packing plant.

Shellabarger Grain Tower

The Shellabarger Grain Tower is nothing more than a tall silo now, but it was once part of a much larger plant originally owned by David Shellabarger. For a time, the plant produced and sold the corn grits that were used in manufacturing alcohol until prohibition put a stop to that. All production was halted completely when the flourmill attached to the tall grain tower caught fire and burned down in 1923. The cause of the fire was never discovered, but several workers died in the blaze. They attempted to take refuge in the sturdy grain tower, but didn't survive. Interestingly, the castle like grain tower is the only portion of the original plant to still stand today, so it's too bad it didn't provide the safety the doomed men thought it would. Many folks believe the spirits of the three men are forever trapped in the tower they now haunt. People who have experienced paranormal activity there have reported hearing screaming coming from inside the empty tower, and a few select individuals have even felt the touch of unseen hands. One man even reported being pushed down a flight of stone stairs leading to the basement below the tower. The perplexing thing was that there was no one there in the tower who could have pushed the man. Needless to say, he never returned again!

Millikin University

Milliken University was established in the early 1900s by James Milliken. While the school is known for its academic excellence and rich campus life, there is a whole other side to Milliken that keeps people coming back for more. Over the years the college has developed quite a reputation for its alleged hauntings. Buildings like the Albert Taylor Theater, the old gym, Aston Hall, Blackburn Hall, the Alumni House, and the Tri-Delta House are all reportedly haunted.

The Albert Taylor Theater

The most popular ghost on campus resides in the Albert Taylor Theater, located inside Shilling Hall. A little girl, who has been dubbed the "Rail Girl" by students and staff alike, haunts the theater. The young apparition seems to have gotten the name because of her penchant for appearing along the balcony railings of the theater's upper sections. Before any performance in the theater, most thespians leave three pieces of candy out for her. When they forget, the Rail Girl has been known to ruin performances by causing lighting and equipment failures. She's also broken props and injured performers as they are getting ready to step onstage. The girl's presence has also been noted by the sound of her footsteps and an occasional soft cry. It isn't exactly clear who the real Rail Girl might be or how the story got started, but one thing's for sure—if you plan to perform in the Albert Taylor Theater, you better come prepared with three pieces of candy.

The Old Gymnasium

Millikin's Old Gymnasium is another extremely haunted site on campus. It hasn't been used for athletics since the construction of the much newer Griswold Physical Education Center, but interestingly enough, the former gym is now used as a storage facility for theater props—some of which may even include many of the props broken by "Rail Girl" over the years.

It doesn't seem to matter, however, that the gym no longer hosts sporting events...because you can still *hear* the sounds of sporting events going on in the old building. Students, staff, and security guards have all heard the pounding of sprinters rounding the indoor track circling above the court below. And all the sounds of an intense basketball game can be heard as well... from sneakers sliding across the polished court in sync with the dribbling of the leather basketball against it, to the referee's whistle and the crowd's claps and cheers. Anyone standing outside the gymnasium might assume there was either a basketball game or a track meet taking place when, in reality, the building's interior was really desolate. No one has determined a cause for the paranormal occurrences. Some folks speculate that electrical disturbances are playing tricks with people's minds, while others suggest the underground lake upon which the gym rests has something to do with the strange activity. Whatever the cause, it seems some of the school's alumni have stuck around in the old gym.

The Dormitories

Many of the residential dorms, including the women's dormitories–Blackburn and Ashton Halls–are haunted.

The ghost of a former female student who jumped to her death from the window of her upper floor dorm room haunts Blackburn Hall. The reason for her suicide has been lost in the shuffle of time, but her old room is readily identified by the conspicuous window that has been covered with alternative bricks that differ from the rest of the building.

In Ashton Hall, which happens to be attached to Blackburn Hall, resides another female spirit whose identity is known. The building is haunted by the ghost of Bernice Richardson who wanders the third floor. Ashton Hall is the oldest women's dorm on campus and was the home of Miss Richardson while she was a student there in the 1920s. The girl committed suicide in her dorm room by ingesting poisonous carbolic acid obtained from one of the science labs after her grades dropped so severely that she was to be kicked out of school. Rather than suffer the humiliation of her academic fate, she chose a new fate and ended her own life. Now she'll *never* have to leave Milliken and is resigned to haunting the halls of Ashton...where she's been seen passing through walls and roaming from room to room, slamming doors and knocking on walls. Her ghostly image is said to be so ghastly that the third floor was even closed off for several years in the 1930s. Apparently, there are burns around her mouth where the acid began eating away at her flesh and completely consumed her lips, forming a sinister expression.

She's not one to mess with either...as she's been known to *bite* residents hard enough to leave a mark.

The Tri-Delta and Alumni Houses

The Alumni House was formerly the home of the Greek organization Zeta Tau Alpha, which named a room in the house after its resident ghost "Louise," who was the Mueller family maid when they owned the house prior to it becoming a campus staple. Louise is relatively harmless and doesn't make a full appearance often, but she can be heard walking about opening and closing doors as she goes.

The Tri-Delta House, home to the Delta Delta Delta Sorority, has its own ghosts. The house was built on top of the Miller family cemetery, although the cemetery may have been in such ruins at the time the site was initially chosen that no one realized it until they began digging up bones and old headstones. The upheaval of the Miller cemetery may have contributed to the current hauntings in the house as evidenced by the 1800s era clothing worn by the female apparition most often seen and heard in the house.

☠☠☠☠☠

The hauntings mentioned here are some of the more renowned ones on campus, although there have been reports of paranormal activity in many other locations as well. If you plan on checking out any of them, your best bets are the old gym, the theater, and Ashton Hall. The strong spectral presences at those three sites are sure to get your adrenaline racing and your heart pumping.

Decatur's Graveyards

Peck Cemetery

One of the most interesting cemeteries in the entire state of Illinois is hidden away in a small town about twenty minutes from Decatur. A lot of cemeteries are associated with ghost sightings and paranormal activity—after all, being the final resting place for countless souls, they are a prime place for spirits to surface. Yet there are many sleepy cemeteries that quietly exist without so much as the sound of the wind whistling through. Peck Cemetery is *not* one of them.

The spirit activity at Peck Cemetery is reputed to rival that of the infamous Bachelor's Grove Cemetery in Midlothian, Illinois. But wandering ghosts are the least of your worries should you dare to venture inside the cemetery after dark. Occult activity and an ominous "devil's chair" have been the source of some extremely unsettling occurrences—even *death*.

Some of the strange activity associated with the cemetery includes unidentified apparitions, cloaked figures, strange cries, unexplained voices, and glowing lights. And the temperature inside the confines of the iron-fence-enclosed cemetery always tends to be several degrees cooler than that of the surrounding area.

Visiting the cemetery after dark can even leave you stranded. There have been numerous incidents of automobiles not starting once the after-hours visitor has gone inside. In fact, legend has it that if you pull your car through the iron gates and into the cemetery's perimeter at night...it won't start again until morning. Now, unless you want to spend the night with restless spirits and strong, negative energies you might think twice before parking your car anywhere near the cemetery.

Well-known local ghost author and investigator Troy Taylor tells of a similar experience. Taylor and his friends decided to investigate Peck Cemetery for themselves one rainy night. They drove their vehicle all the way up to the cemetery's entrance, but didn't pull the car inside past the gate. They exited the illusive safety of the vehicle, leaving the headlights on. The bright lights pierced the thick darkness that shrouded the cemetery grounds and whatever else might be lurking inside. But as brightly as those headlights shined, it wasn't enough to illuminate the entire cemetery and darkness still surrounded them.

Nervously, Taylor and his buddies trudged ahead, braving the darkness. A coolness ran through the cemetery as rain dripped through the looming trees...but they pressed on. They finally reached the farthest perimeter of the cemetery—WITHOUT incident. *No* mysterious sounds, *no* ghosts, *no* floating lights — nothing. Not one creepy thing occurred...that is, until they turned and started walking back.

As Taylor and his friends made their way back through the cemetery, trotting across the damp ground, graves underfoot, the mood lightened. The anticipation of a good scare gone unfulfilled was met with relief. They had made it across the cemetery grounds safely. But just as they were nearing the main gate, the *unexplained* happened. The car's headlights that had shined so fiercely through the murky shadows, without explanation, suddenly flashed off and everyone was left standing in the stark blackness of the secluded cemetery.

No one knew what to make of it. Maybe the battery had died, in which case the long standing legend of cars not starting until morning had just come to pass. They just might be sleeping amongst the unknown in the cemetery after all. But luckily for Taylor and his friends, the vehicle started without fail. The headlights even turned back on with the pull of the knob on the retro-style dashboard. As soon as they were all safely back in the car, you can be sure they tore out of there like a bat out of hell.

Taylor and his compadres enjoyed a good fright and walked out of there with a great story, but others have not been so lucky. An Occult leader placed a curse on the cemetery back in the 1970s when satanic rituals were reportedly performed there, including animal sacrifices and black magic. They even went so far as to vandalize the cemetery, destroying various graves in the process.

As part of the ritual ceremonies, the leader of the cult group placed a chair in an area of the cemetery where he would sit during the performance. It wasn't just any chair, though. It was known as the *devil's chair*. Anyone who sat in the chair, other than the cult leader, could expect to die within a year thanks to a curse he placed on it. Allegedly, that's exactly what happened to one high school athlete who found the allure of the devil's chair to tempting to resist—legend has it that this popular high school star athlete, who had everything going for him, hanged himself for no clear reason. No one could figure out why someone seemingly so happy and outgoing would do such a thing, but his closest friends knew a secret. Exactly *one year* prior to his apparent suicide, the young athlete had visited Peck Cemetery and dared to sit in the devil's chair. Stories of other students suffering a similar fate began to leak out as well so it seems the curse was real.

If you were thinking of trying the devil's chair out for yourself, you're out of luck. At some point the local sheriff elected to put a stop to all the curiosity seekers and made arrangements to remove the chair from Peck Cemetery. It was no easy task, though. Despite its small size, the chair was not easily removed. Sledgehammers were used, bulldozers brought in, and eventually explosives. Initially, officials managed to remove only the arms and back of the chair, leaving just the pedestal shaped seat.

If all these stories aren't enough to scare you away, take your chances and explore the cemetery for yourself — if you dare! It's not easy to find, though. Many would-be ghost hunters have gotten lost searching for this elusive cemetery. The area has changed so dramatically over the years that the directions provided by cemetery enthusiasts of days past are no longer accurate. Old gravel roads have long since been paved over to accommodate the slowly developing area, and the cemetery seems to have slipped into the background and out of sight. But you can try and find it off Donavan Road beyond the small sleepy town of Cerro Gordo. Just know, that despite its isolated appearance, the cemetery is not empty and you won't be alone should you choose to go in. And if you don't believe me, you might try checking in with the Ghost Haunters, a group of paranormal investigators of Illinois. They've captured the image of a male apparition peering inside the cemetery from over the old weathered fence that surrounds it.

☠☠☠☠☠

Greenwood Cemetery

What would you think if you were out fishing along the local river, a quiet activity you've done many times before, and you suddenly spotted several caskets floating past, some even washing ashore? That would certainly be a strange and unexpected experience. It would also seem to be an unlikely one, but a full century ago that's exactly what happened.

Where did the floating caskets come from? In the early 1900s, Decatur's Sangamon River overflowed after some heavy rainstorms ripped through the area. The river ran along the south end of Greenwood Cemetery, one of the oldest cemeteries in all of Decatur. The overflowing river flooded all nearby low-lying areas, including a portion of Greenwood Cemetery—and it was so severe that the headstones of several graves were toppled to the ground. But even worse was the dislodging of actual caskets that had long been buried. The extensive flooding forced many of them up out of their graves... only to be carried away down the river by the rushing waters. Now that truly would have been a sight to see.

Once as many of the caskets had been recovered from the river as possible, they were reburied in another area of the cemetery. It was not possible to identify some of the caskets and bodies, so many of them were buried together in common graves and went unmarked. Ever since the disruption and reburial of these graves, cemetery visitors have reported strange unexplained lights dancing around that area of the cemetery where the graves had been disturbed by the flood. Without warning, the lights appear out of nowhere. They playfully dance around for a while before vanishing into the darkness. To this day, those lights continue to be seen by many and are believed to be the restless spirits of those unearthed during the flood.

There's a long history to Greenwood Cemetery that includes other paranormal activity besides just the mysterious lights floating around the cemetery's southern end. There have been sightings of a ghostly bride, phantom funerals, and an unidentified female apparition near a spooky staircase. There even used to be a haunted mausoleum in the cemetery's earlier days.

The cemetery grounds predate the establishment of Decatur when the Illiniwek Indians first used them as burial grounds. At the time, villages were scattered about in outlying areas of what is now Decatur. None were actually located on any of the land Decatur now occupies. In fact, historical documents indicate the entire city of Decatur sits atop sacred Illiniwek burial grounds. Many believe this fact accounts for Decatur being one of the most haunted cities in Illinois. That's certainly one possibility, but much of the supernatural activity in the cemetery can be traced back to other causes.

One of the most legendary ghosts of Greenwood is a young bride who's been walking the cemetery grounds since the final years of the prohibition era in the early 1930s. The young woman's plight is somewhat of a Romeo and Juliet story. She was involved with a young man who sold illegal whiskey in the bootlegging business. The woman's parents did not approve of their daughter's involvement with him and forbidded them from marrying. The deeply enamored couple couldn't bear to be apart and decided to elope behind her parent's back.

On the evening of the night they were to elope, the young man needed to deliver a final batch of whiskey before he could meet up with his beloved. The money he would earn from this last bootlegging transaction would be used to marry and provide for his bride. They decided upon a place to meet later that night. In the meantime, the young woman would wait at home while her husband to be went about his business.

When it was time for the two young lovers to meet up, the woman prepared to leave her parent's house unnoticed. She carefully put on the wedding dress she had hidden in the back of her closet and snuck off to meet her beau. She waited for a while at the designated meeting place, but her sweetheart didn't come. She thought perhaps he had been delayed in delivering the whiskey, so she continued waiting. Still, he did not come. By morning it was clear he wasn't coming. Had he stood her up? The young woman didn't know what to think, but she knew she had to hurry home before her parents noticed she'd been gone all night.

Later that following day, while quietly waiting at home for word from her betrothed, she finally found out why he had never arrived the night before. He had been murdered! When the young man went to deliver the illicit whiskey and collect payment, he was killed by some fellow bootleggers who stole his whiskey. They tossed his lifeless body into the Sangamon River that runs along the south end of Greenwood Cemetery. The story doesn't end there, though.

Upon hearing the news of her beloved's death, the young woman became so distraught that her parents had to call for a doctor. Reportedly, the doctor prescribed a mild sedative to help calm the heartbroken young woman. Her parents were relieved as the sedative began to kick in and their daughter seemed to be feeling a little better. Their minds were put at ease, but that wouldn't last. When they went to check on their daughter in her room later that night, they discovered that she had disappeared. Had the bootleggers who murdered her boyfriend come after her as well? The distressed parents spent the rest of the evening anxiously awaiting their daughter's return, but it wasn't to be.

The following morning, their daughter's body was discovered floating face down in the very same river in which two fishermen had previously found the body of her beau. Had the young woman suffered the same fate as her boyfriend at the hands of the murdering bootleggers? At first glance that might seem to be the case. However, as it turns out, the young woman could not bear the thought of living without her love. It seems the sedatives prescribed by the doctor were not enough to ease the woman's immense pain. She drowned herself in the Sangamon River right where her boyfriend's body had been so callously tossed by his killers. When the young woman's parents prepared to bury their daughter, in her closet they discovered the wedding dress she had planned to wear for the secret wedding ceremony she and her beloved had wanted so badly. They clothed their daughter in the wedding dress for burial.

The heartbroken woman now wears her wedding dress for eternity as she wanders the grounds of Greenwood Cemetery, her final "resting" place. Countless witnesses have spotted her many times over the years wandering the hillside where her grave is located. Perhaps, in death, she hopes to reunite with and finally marry her true love. Until she finds him, her restless soul may continue searching and Greenwood will continue to have a phantom bride.

The Greenwood Bride is not the only woman to wander the cemetery grounds. Another female specter has also been observed in the northwest portion of the cemetery where a peculiar set of steps stand alone against a gently sloping hillside. These steps are often referred to as the Barrackman staircase, although it isn't really a full staircase. There are actually only five small steps leading from the winding cemetery road that wraps around the slight hillside to a cluster of four graves atop the hill directly in front of the staircase. The four graves are perfectly aligned side by side in a straight row and marked by nearly identical rectangular headstones, slightly rounded at the top, all bearing the name "Barrackman." The Barrackmans included Mr. and Mrs. Barrackman, as well as their son and his wife.

Not much is known about the Barrackmans, but their name is well known among cemetery visitors. Many of them have even caught a glimpse of either Mrs. Barrackman or her daughter-in-law sitting on the short staircase leading up to their final resting place. No one is certain which of the two ladies it is, but an ethereal female figure in a long gown is often spotted sitting on the steps looking down, as though sad. She only appears at sundown, and immediately disappears once the sun has completely set. Visitors still in the cemetery as the sun begins to set just may catch a glimpse of this somber spirit as she makes a brief appearance before returning to her grave.

Greenwood Cemetery also once hosted a grand mausoleum. Built in 1908, the Greenwood Mausoleum would become a popular final resting place for many of Decatur's finest residents until it was eventually torn down in 1967. There are many individuals who believe that tearing down the once great mausoleum and displacing the bodies of those who were at rest there has left some of those souls now in a state of unrest. In the area where the mausoleum once stood at the bottom of a headstone speckled hillside, witnesses have reported hearing strange sounds and chilly temperatures even in the midst of summer. Unexplained paranormal occurrences have also been experienced at the site of a common grave just across the cemetery roadway from where the mausoleum used to be. Several unidentified bodies that were removed from the mausoleum prior to its demolition were placed in this common grave. The souls of the individuals to whom those bodies belonged may not have appreciated being disturbed and displaced. That would explain all the strange activity that was observed by paranormal investigators studying the site of the common grave in the summer of 1996.

While the destruction of the Greenwood Mausoleum seems to have produced quite a bit of supernatural activity, strange happenings were already occurring in and around the mausoleum even when it was still standing. Many mausoleum visitors reported hearing hushed whispers and unknown voices inside, as well as unexplained screams. Interestingly, the reason the mausoleum was torn down was due to irreparable damage. The building had deteriorated to such an extent, possibly due to repeated exposure to inclement weather over the years, that the decision was made to tear it down. Perhaps the decaying conditions didn't sit well with the souls within and they became restless, letting out an occasional cry or moan to show their disapproval for the lack of upkeep. Whatever the cause, the area of the cemetery associated with the mausoleum exhibits some strong paranormal activity. But, then again, paranormal occurrences are common throughout all of Greenwood Cemetery...especially phantom funerals.

Phantom funerals are funeral processions or gatherings like any other...except for the fact that everyone in attendance is a ghost! There have been several sightings of funeral parties mourning the loss of a loved one graveside before the entire groups just vanishes completely into thin air. One of the most interesting sightings was observed by a man visiting the cemetery on a sunny afternoon. As he walked through the cemetery on his way to pay his respects to a lost loved one, he spotted a funeral party gathered around another grave up on a hill. Not wanting to disturb them, he waited out of sight before venturing up the hill to his destination. To his surprise, the funeral party was nowhere to be seen. As he strolled up the slight hill and neared the grave around which they had been gathered, he failed to spot any newly dug open grave as would normally be expected. Instead, what he did notice was the date on the headstone of the only grave located in that spot. The date of the person's passing matched the current day, only the year was dated sixty years prior. Had the man just witnessed a replaying of a funeral that first took place sixty years ago? It would seem so.

Others have had similar experiences in Greenwood Cemetery. Another instance involved a member of the cemetery grounds crew. As he was grooming the lawn, he observed a funeral party in the cemetery. Strange, he thought, since no funerals were scheduled to take place at Greenwood that particular day. What was even more curious was that, despite the year being relatively recent, all of the automobiles parked along the cemetery path were 1930s and '40s era models, like a shiny black Buick Roadmaster, a Lincoln Zephyr, or a Chrysler Windsor. When the worker finished what he was doing, he went to share the interesting sighting with a fellow co-worker. The co-worker hadn't noticed the funeral party or the period cars. The two men checked the schedule for the day and discovered there were no funerals planned. What the cemetery worker had witnessed was a phantom funeral. There are many more tales of phantom funerals in Greenwood Cemetery—too many to tell in fact. If we covered them all, we'd never get out of the cemetery. Before we conclude our walk through Greenwood Cemetery, there are a few more ghosts to see... ghosts of Civil War soldiers.

Remember the flooding of the Sangamon River and the floating caskets? Some of those graves that were disturbed during the flooding belonged to soldiers of the Civil War, both Union and Confederate. Illinois was, of course, on the side of the Union and against slavery. Many Union soldiers who lost their lives during the war were ultimately buried in Decatur's Greenwood Cemetery. And, although they probably wouldn't appreciate it, they were sometimes buried next to their Confederate counterparts. Now why would this be?

Whenever the Union had captured Confederate soldiers, they would transport them by train to Camp Douglas, a prison camp beyond Chicago. During one particular trip to the prison camp, many southern soldiers died from disease. Not wanting to transport the dead soldiers with the living, the train stopped near Decatur and unloaded the deceased prisoners whose bodies were transported to Greenwood Cemetery. They were quickly buried on a steep hillside within the cemetery. Worse than the hasty burial, lack of funeral, and nothing to mark the graves was the possibility that not all of the soldiers were actually dead. There were so many gravely ill Confederate soldiers aboard the train that it was difficult to tell which ones had already passed and which were barely still hanging on by a thread. When all of the bodies were transported to the cemetery, it's very possible that some were still alive when pulled off the train and subsequently buried. And it makes sense that suffering a fate as terrifying as to be buried alive would be cause for haunting activity.

Reports of supernatural activity in that area of the cemetery have included whispers, cries, and footsteps, as well as sightings of ghostly soldiers wearing ragged Civil War period military uniforms wandering amongst the graves. Some witnesses have even felt the brush of unseen hands across their backs. Some of this activity could be the result of Confederate soldiers having been buried alive. Or it could be due to the flooding of that portion of the cemetery when the Sangamon River overflowed. When the Confederate soldiers were buried, they had been quickly tossed into shallow graves along the side of the steep hill. All it took were heavy rains softening the hillside earth to slowly extricate the bodies until subsequent flooding dislodged them completely. But it wasn't just Confederate soldiers whose bodies were displaced by the flooding—the graves of many Union soldiers were disturbed as well.

After the rains ceased and the flooding had gone down, cemetery staff worked to recover whatever remains they could. Unfortunately, the bodies could no longer be identified due to years of decay. And for the Confederate soldiers, no records had ever been kept on any of them anyway so they would continue to remain unknown. All the recovered remains, whether Union or Confederate soldiers, were reburied together in an area dedicated to memorializing soldiers of the Civil War. Many of the graves are marked "unknown U.S. Soldier." Greenwood visitors who have spotted spectral soldiers in that portion of the cemetery are convinced many of the men haunt the area because they don't know where they are. As time goes on and surroundings change, they will surely only become more disoriented and continue to wander the grounds looking for the path home.

The Common Burial Grounds

Decatur's original graveyard has a simple name, the Common Burial Grounds. The cemetery used to overlap with another one by the name of King's Cemetery. Since they were right next to one another, most folks just ended up grouping them together and calling the entire place the Common Burial Grounds. Due to overcrowding, the cemetery was officially closed in 1885 and the land was divided and sold to the city of Decatur for new development. The bodies of those once buried there were relocated to the much larger Greenwood Cemetery. Regrettably, not all of the bodies made the trip over. As digging commenced for the development of new homes and businesses, various bones were unearthed—and they continue to be discovered on occasion to this day. There are even reports of people not only finding bones, but also broken scraps from coffins. Full skeletons have even been encountered. Other than being a bit off-putting, much of this might have seemed relatively benign except for the residual hauntings the unearthing of bones seemed to cause.

Though it no longer stands, Decatur's legendary Blue Mill Restaurant—erected upon these grounds—has not been forgotten. In its day, it was reputed to be haunted by the spirits of those whose bones lay beneath. Employees often reported strange activity occurring there...such as ghostly figures manifesting, strange sounds, and relocated objects. A new business now stands on the spot where the Blue Mill once served hungry customers, but many believe the spirits are still there and that the hauntings haven't stopped.

Wabash Train Station & Railroad

Our final destination on this haunted trip through Decatur takes us down the dusty tracks of the old train station and the once busy railways running past it. Here, murder, decapitation, and a broken heart all converge, and the spirit world collides with our own. And so begins our story of Decatur's haunted Wabash train station.

Wabash Station was built in 1869 at the height of railroad expansion across the Midwest. The station became a central point through which trains passed from St. Louis to Chicago and beyond. All types of people traveled to and from Decatur on a daily basis, including such prominent individuals as President Abraham Lincoln, who arrived by train for the Republican Convention in 1860. It certainly was an exciting time.

But, perhaps, even more exciting than the many people passing through at the time are the ones who have lingered behind long after they should have been gone. No longer used for commuters, the only activity on the railways these days comes from the slow chugging of heavy freight trains passing by. With the decline of commuter activity, the station was abandoned. But restoration efforts have since revamped the almost forgotten building and it now operates, quite appropriately, as an antique store. And even though you can't buy a ride on the next train these days, the original ticket window still stands, as do the smooth wood floors and many of the benches.

Imagine you are working at the grand Wabash train station during its prime. You're the only person scheduled during the evening hours and so you spend your time dusting the benches and sweeping the floor. The ticket window is closed and there are no scheduled passenger train arrivals or departures. There really shouldn't be anyone else in the station during that late hour, but out of the corner of your eye you spot a lonely woman dressed all in white sitting quietly on one of the benches. You glance over at her and she appears to be anxious. You don't want to bother her, so you continue sweeping, but when you look up again a moment later...she is *gone*. She has completely vanished.

There have been numerous sightings of this unusual woman in white. Several different station workers have spotted her over the years. Each time the woman has disappeared just as suddenly as she appeared, leaving the unsuspecting witness completely baffled. On one occasion, an employee was cleaning the women's restroom. No one else was in there and the station was fairly empty at the time. As the female employee went about her cleaning duties, she heard the restroom door open...and the sweet scent of perfume wafted inside. When the employee looked up, no one was there, but the room was filled with a fragrant floral aroma. A chill ran through her body—she had not seen anyone enter or leave the restroom and was sure she had just had a brief brush with the mysterious woman in white. But the lone woman in white is not without help in her haunting. There is another spirit or two roaming around the station as well; they are identified by a strange light that can sometimes be seen floating along the old tracks.

So what could be causing all the strange phenomena at the station?

Long ago, when the station was bustling with activity, many a soldier departed from the Wabash Station, leaving behind family, on their way to fight in the raging First World War. One lucky wife received news that her husband would finally be returning home from the war. After being away for several months, he sent her a telegram with the exciting news. He told her when to expect him by train. She couldn't wait for the day of his arrival. When the day finally came, she hurried down to the grand station to meet him...only he never arrived.

She sat patiently waiting all day to no avail. When the last commuter train had passed through for the day, it was clear he would not be home that day. The disappointed wife assumed her husband had been delayed and had just not had a chance to contact her. She simply decided to return to the station again the next day. With each train that stopped in Decatur, she eagerly watched for her beloved...but he still didn't arrive. For a full week the poor wife worried that her husband had been sent back to the warfront. Then she finally received a telegram indicating he had not returned to war. Unfortunately, he would not be returning home either. On the way to catch a train from New York to Decatur, the bus he was riding in crashed and he was killed. The horrible news was more than the woman could bear. She swallowed a fistful of pills and went to sleep...never to wake up again.

Based on the numerous sightings of a woman dressed in white waiting for a train that would never arrive, it seems the soldier and his wife have still been unable to reunite even in death.

Rather than move on to whatever was awaiting her in death, the woman continued to haunt the old train station watching for her husband. Perhaps his ghost is wandering the streets of New York at the site of his bus accident searching for his wife. Until these two finally reunite, the woman in white will continue waiting, giving the rest of us who visit the old station a chill.

While that explains the ghostly woman, what about that strange light shining along the train tracks? There are two equally horrifying explanations for the source of that unidentified light, both paranormal in nature. The light has been observed on numerous occasions; it appears out of nowhere and is never traced back to anything. There is no natural explanation for how or why the light shines. There are, however, two *supernatural* explanations...

The downtown area was quite splendid back in the time when the railroads ran busy with daily commuter traffic in and out of Decatur, at least by day anyway. As night fell, things quickly changed. Gambling, drinking, and prostitution transformed the area, giving it an entirely different character. The seedy nightlife gave rise to the need for additional patrol in all areas, including the train station.

On a brisk October morning in 1935, despite an officer on duty patrolling the train station, a brutal crime was committed that has remained unsolved and forever leaving a permanent imprint upon the place. Two men rushed to jump onto a passenger train, seemingly without tickets. Their suspicious behavior caught the attention of patrolman Omer Davenport who attempted to apprehend them. The two men were clearly on the run for something serious and couldn't risk capture so, using a .32 caliber handgun, they started shooting before escaping—never to be seen again.

Officer Davenport had been patrolling the railways for six years as a Wabash Railroad Police Officer. Prior to that, he was the Decatur Chief of Police for four years after having served in the military and fighting in World War I. Davenport was an experienced officer, but he took a bullet that day. Wounded, but still alive, he was rushed to the nearby Wabash Employees Hospital where he was treated for gunshot wounds to the leg and throat. Doctors only needed to remove the bullets and Davenport would likely recover. Unfortunately, it was decided that operating on the throat was too risky and the surgery wasn't performed. The bullet in his throat eventually worked its way down into the officer's lungs and he took a turn for the worse. Later that same night Davenport died.

Losing his life in the line of duty at the Wabash Train Station that day didn't necessarily stop Officer Davenport from continuing to patrol the railways, though. From time to time a bright light, not unlike that of the large flashlight carried by Davenport on patrol, is seen shining along the tracks that still run past the Wabash Train Station. Officer Davenport is apparently determined to continue his patrol of the station and railways, as was his duty.

But that's not the only place Davenport could be seen wandering after his death. Before the Wabash Employees Hospital building, where Davenport ultimately died, was torn down in 1996, his ghost was often observed wandering the halls. Even in later years, long after the staff who had treated Davenport's gunshot wounds would have been gone, there were sightings of an unidentified man aimlessly walking the halls before suddenly disappearing. Staff descriptions of this man closely matched Officer Davenport, and these were coming from staff members who had never before seen him!

A final tragedy on the rails involves the decapitation of an unknown trainman who worked the brakes by walking along the top of the train and turning the brake wheel on each car while the train was still in motion. Sounds like a dangerous job, but someone had to do it or the train couldn't stop. The trainman, or brakeman as they were often called, also assisted the conductor by signaling when it was all clear to depart. The brakeman carried a lantern and flashed it toward the front of the train to alert the conductor that it was either safe to move or that there was a potential problem.

Anytime the train would roll into town, stopping at the local station, it was the brakeman's duty to inspect the wheels of each car, as well as the couplings joining one car to the next. The conductor would be notified of any potential problems so that they could be corrected prior to departing again. Since it was usually a long walk from the rear of the train to the front, brakemen saved time by waving a lantern toward the train's engine where the conductor sat rather than walking all the way down. Shining the lantern a certain way signaled there was a problem.

On one particular occasion, when a train had stopped at the Wabash Station in Decatur, the brakeman performed his usual duties. He hopped off the train and proceeded to check all the wheels and couplings of each train car. The alert brakeman observed a potential problem, possibly with the coupling between two cars. He bent down to take a look, but as he peered beneath the train, it began to move slightly. There was no time to get out of the way and he was knocked off balance, dropping his lantern to the ground in the process. Before he could get up, he was caught between two cars.

The fallen lantern caught the attention of others nearby who ran to help, but there was nothing they could do. They were too late. As one car of the train jammed forward into the other, the brakeman's head was chopped clean off. Legend has it that, initially, no one realized his head had been severed from his body. Since he was caught beneath the train it was difficult to see what had happened. Several men pulled the brakeman from under the train and carried him into the station, only unknowingly carrying just his body. His head was left behind.

From time to time, it's still possible to see the light of the brakeman's lantern bouncing along tracks and the platform of the train station. There have been countless sightings of this light shining along the rails in the midst of nothingness without a natural cause. This mysterious light has yet to be traced back to a tangible spotlight, flashlight, or other source. The only explanation for the bouncing light is the phantom lantern of the decapitated brakeman who seems to be stuck working the rails indefinitely. But maybe it isn't freight cars he's inspecting. Perhaps he's looking for his severed head!

5

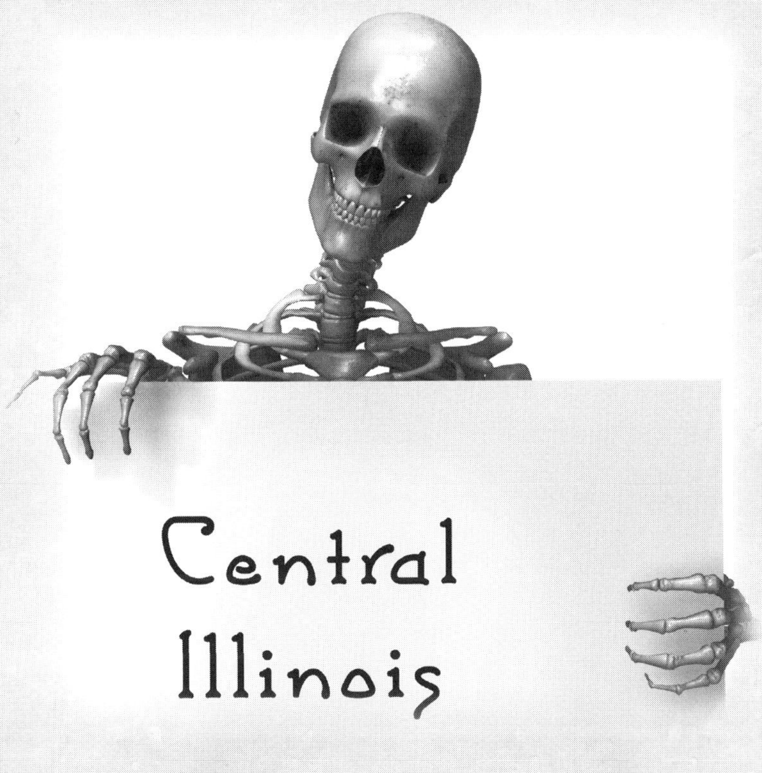

Central Illinois

Central Illinois

The central Illinois area surrounding the cities of Springfield and Decatur is full of many of its own haunted locations as well. This region of the state is especially laden with a handful of haunted cemeteries and boasts several haunted colleges. Between the University of Illinois at Champaign-Urbana, Eastern Illinois University in Charleston, and Illinois College in Jacksonville, who knew there were so many campuses plagued by paranormal activity? And all the long-standing little cemeteries sprinkled about can only enhance the presence of ghosts throughout the region.

Voorhies Castle

The small central Illinois town of Voorhies is in close proximity to Decatur, less than thirty miles east of it. There you'll find an interesting castle-like home in the midst of Amish country. The original owner of the castle was a Swedish immigrant named Nels Larson, who acquired the undeveloped property from another man named William Voorhies, for whom the town is named. Larson had the castle house built in a chalet style reminiscent of his Swedish roots. Two tall towers on either side of the home gave it the appearance of a castle. The house sat on an expansive property accompanied by a large barn. A few years after building his impressive home, Larson decided to construct an enormous clock tower, which would take over five years to complete, that would ultimately be connected to the barn. The addition of the clock tower that stood about twice as tall as the attached barn gave the ensemble a look resembling that of a chapel.

Larson lived in the home with his wife Johannah and their two children. All was well until Johannah collapsed unexpectedly one day and was found dead by one of the servants. Following his wife's untimely death, Larson moved out of the home and never returned. The grand castle was just too strong a reminder of what he'd lost. Had he not left he may have been able to enjoy her company for the remainder of his years...as her ghost is said to haunt her old homestead, often looking out one of the tower windows. In the years following her death, visitors to the castle reported hearing her gentle footsteps softly walking throughout the house and she was even known to turn lights on and off, play various notes on the piano, and even open locked windows.

In death, husband and wife might finally have been reunited when the spirit of Nels Larson found its way back to their beloved home. It's been said that at the exact moment of his death the clock tower on the barn struck thirteen times. Even though Larson no longer lived in the house, he had such a strong connection with the property and especially his treasured clock tower that it rang out in recognition of his passing. For as long as the clock tower stood tall above the barn, it continued to ring thirteen times every year on the anniversary of his death, March 29. Many believe the clock would still chime thirteen times every March if it hadn't been destroyed by a violent tornado in 1976. But though it no longer stands, some folks claim you can still hear the distinct sound of the clock ringing out across the property of the Voorhies Castle on the anniversary of its master's death each year.

In addition to the house being haunted by Mrs. Larson, and possibly her husband, there is a strange story about the castle that points to a third possible source for the hauntings. It is, by far, the most interesting story associated with the home, but it's not an easy one to verify. Nels and Johannah Larson were known to have had two children, George and Ellen. However, some family accounts suggest they might have had a third child. If that were true, how come no one ever knew about the child? Allegedly, out of shame, the child was hidden away in the house and kept a secret because of severe mental retardation. The child is reputed to have been confined to a small room somewhere in the house, and possibly even chained to the wall to keep him or her from running about the house where prying eyes might see. Years after the Larson family no longer occupied the house various visitors reported hearing the sound of clattering chains coming from somewhere deep in the house. The source of the eerie sounds has never been traced and many believe the noise to be an indication of the presence of the poor child's spirit still trapped in the house. We may never know the real story behind this mysterious family, but some psychics who have visited the property have opted not to enter the house because of the strong negative vibes given off there.

Ghostly Cemeteries

Chesterville Cemetery

Slightly southeast of Decatur is the tiny town of Chesterville, originally settled by Amish and Mennonite groups. The town is so small that its population isn't even displayed on the Chesterville sign denoting arrival in this sleepy little town. On first glance, there might not seem to be anything remarkable about this quiet place, but a trip to the most solitary location within this town will reveal some unexpected surprises. The Chesterville Cemetery is simple enough and doesn't necessarily see much traffic, but there is a strange sight within that has been a source of curiosity for anyone who happens to stumble upon it. Along the edge of the cemetery bordering the Kaskaskia River stands an isolated large oak tree. What makes this old oak strange is that it's surrounded on all sides by a short iron fence. The fence is decorated all around with pointed spindles jutting sharply upward, preventing anyone from sitting or stepping on top of the fence without risk of injury. There is also a stone grave marker that has been worn down with the passing years so that the name that once graced it is no longer visible, but that might be for the best. The more than one hundred-year-old grave is said to be the final resting place of a witch.

Allegedly, sometime during the early 1900s, a local woman who disagreed with the Amish church's stance on several important issues boldly voiced her dissent. The Chesterville community was shocked by her apparent betrayal of their long-held beliefs. No one had ever expressed such divergent views before, nor could they fathom anyone disagreeing with the church. There must be some explanation for this woman's unacceptable behavior. Ultimately, an investigation into the matter resulted in the woman being accused of witchery. In order to protect the community, she would have to be sacrificed—as was common practice with convicted witches in those days. Following the woman's execution, the town buried her body in the local cemetery. In order to ensure she would no longer cause any trouble, they planted a tree over the top of her grave with the hope of trapping her there. They didn't want her evil spirit returning from the dead to avenge her own death through the use of witchcraft. The old oak tree may not have been enough to

keep her down, however, as there have been occasional sightings of the woman's ghost lingering around the fenced tree.

While that certainly is an intriguing story about the female apparition that is sometimes spotted near the old oak, there is an alternate explanation for who she was that counters the sordid story of witchcraft. You might consider the first account to be that of the wicked witch, while the second pays homage to a good witch. This second story dates back to the 1800s and centers on a young woman revered for her mystical healing powers. She had a remarkable ability to heal others, and was as equally impressive in her uncanny connection with nature and wildlife. People often sought this woman's healing touch when gravely ill so you can imagine the grief upon her passing. When she died, her father was said to have planted the oak graveside so that her benevolent spirit could live on through the mighty tree that would sprout there.

Ridge Cemetery

Ridge Cemetery is located near the town of Tower Hill south of Decatur. The cemetery itself actually sits upon Williamsburg Hill, and was once part of the town of Williamsburg. Unfortunately for the small town that was established in 1839, Williamsburg eventually dropped off the map in the 1880s when railroad transportation cropped up everywhere else but there. With no easy way in and out of Williamsburg people moved on and the town faded into obscurity. Williamsburg Hill, however, has persisted all these years due to bouts of supernatural activity that have come to be associated with Ridge Cemetery. Over the years, people have reported seeing strange lights, phantom funerals, shadow men, and various apparitions, particularly that of an old man who likes to linger just long enough for onlookers to catch

a quick glimpse before departing into thin air. Reportedly, there has also been occult activity inside the cemetery as evidenced by the discovery of mutilated animal carcasses. This cemetery is just one of countless little known cemeteries throughout the state of Illinois. But unlike most that simply sit quietly, offering a restful way to spend eternity, Ridge Cemetery is very much alive with paranormal activity.

☠☠☠☠☠

Old Union Cemetery

About twenty miles north of Decatur, and over the county line, is the town of Clinton. On the outskirts of Clinton rests a modest cemetery named Old Union. The cemetery was originally associated with Old Union Church, a congregation that had first organized in people's homes in 1831. Their first church was built in 1838 and a second, larger one was constructed directly in front of the cemetery in 1864, but later burned down. Interestingly, the original pastor of the church, Father Hugh Bowles, happened to be an acquaintance of President Abraham Lincoln. Following the pastor's death, the church continued for just a few decades more before eventually being abandoned in favor of relocation to the nearby town of Clinton, which was suddenly flourishing with the arrival of the railroad system.

Despite being left behind, Old Union Cemetery hasn't been forgotten...at least not by the restless spirits lingering there. Both cemetery workers and police officers have reported the presence of unexplained orbs and lights. Other witnesses have experienced chillingly cold temperatures in certain parts of the cemetery when the surrounding temperatures are much warmer.

Peculiar sensations have also been experienced near an unusual grave situated at the back of the cemetery. The grave is marked by a pillar shaped headstone bearing the name Ben Hull and is completely surrounded by a decorative metal fence with intricately laced posts all the way around. A visit to this grave reveals that it has suffered over the years. Vandals, harsh weather, or both have knocked over portions of the fence. The disturbance of the grave may have caused Hull's unrest so that he now haunts his own grave, giving anyone who dares come near a chilly sensation.

College Specters

University of Illinois, Champaign-Urbana

Like many long-standing colleges and universities, the University of Illinois at Champaign-Urbana has had its share of ghost stories. Former students are rumored to haunt numerous buildings on campus. In particular, both the English and Psychology buildings are said to house ghosts, as does the YMCA, which is said to host the spirit of none other than the controversial Chief Illiniwek himself. An apparition has also been spotted looking out a third floor window of Lincoln Hall when the building is otherwise vacant. Incidentally, Lincoln Hall stands in close proximity to the infamously haunted English building.

The story of the haunted YMCA building on Wright Street is likely the most bizarre of them all. The supernatural occurrences there are among the most unexplained on campus and involve a portrait of an Indian Chief that hangs in the basement of the building. On occasion, students and staff in the building after dark have walked by the painting and been startled to see that the Indian Chief was *missing* from it. By morning the painting would once again be intact. Was the spirit of Chief Illiniwek or some other chief roaming the building by night? No one has ever figured out that mystery.

The building that now offers English courses was built in 1905 and was originally used as a women's dorm complete with an indoor pool and gym. It wasn't until 1956 that the building was repurposed for use by the English department. Back when the building was still a women's dorm, a heartbroken student reportedly killed herself in her room over the loss of a boyfriend who had recently broken up with her. Since the woman's tragic death, there have been reports of paranormal activity in various parts of the building, particularly in an office that had formerly been her dorm room. Although the building is no longer recognizable as a dorm, the woman still haunts the hallways of the old building, sometimes slamming doors and causing the lights to flicker on and off.

The Psychology building is also believed to be haunted by a student who unexpectedly died within a few years of contemplating suicide there. Throughout the years, students on campus have noticed traces of ghostly activity in the area of the building where the student once threatened to jump to his death from an upstairs railing overlooking the hard foyer floor below. Students have reported feeling cold spots and hearing phantom footsteps and ghostly whispers when no one is nearby. Those who have experienced the ghost are convinced the deceased student has been cursed with returning to the site of his attempted suicide to live out the moment for all of eternity.

Paranormal activity in the Champaign-Urbana area is not limited to the University of Illinois campus. Not far from there is a small cemetery known as Clements Cemetery. There you'll find a ghost known as the "Blue Man." Sightings of this strange blue hued apparition have only occurred beneath the light of a full moon. The only explanation for why this spirit walks the cemetery by night rather than rest in peace is the unfortunate nature of his death. Records indicate a man was found hanged to death in the woods next to the cemetery sometime during the 1840s. It's not clear whether he was hanged by others and left to die or if he simply committed suicide. Either way, upon discovery, his body was taken down and buried in Clements Cemetery where it remains along with his ghost.

Eastern Illinois University

You probably wouldn't expect the University of Illinois at Champaign-Urbana to be the only haunted campus in Illinois—and you'd be right. About an hour south of the U of I is the town of Charleston and Eastern Illinois University, another haunted campus. When looking for ghosts here, you'll need to visit Pemberton Hall, a women's dorm haunted by the spirit of Mary Hawkins. Mary was a student at Eastern and also a Resident Advisor to other female students in Pemberton Hall. Sometime back in 1917, on a nasty winter night, one of the girls was having a hard time sleeping. Her restlessness prompted her to get up and wander down to the music room where she took a seat at the piano and began playing quietly. While the unsuspecting young woman continued to tickle the ivory keys of the piano, a sinister event was unfolding. A male janitor with keys to the building had let himself in and made his way up to the fourth floor where the insomnia-plagued girl continued playing the piano. As the girl's fingers danced across the smooth white keys, she was grabbed from behind by the janitor, who violently beat her to a bloody pulp, sexually assaulted her, and left her for dead before escaping beneath the dark veil of night. The tenacious young woman roused enough strength to pull herself along the floor, out of the music room, and down the hall to the stairwell. She made it down the stairs leaving a bloody trail behind her and, with the little bit of strength she had left, began scratching at the doors of her fellow Pemberton Hall residents. No one woke to help her though and her cold dead body was found directly outside the door of the resident advisor's room, Mary Hawkins.

The identity of that girl seems to have died with her because in all the tales of the Pemberton Hall hauntings, the murdered girl's name is never uttered. And while many believe the murdered pianist does sometimes still haunt the dorm as the faint sound of a piano can be heard playing up on the now closed off fourth floor, most hauntings are attributed to Mary Hawkins. But why would Mary haunt the dorm when another girl was murdered there? After discovering the dead girl's body, Mary reportedly felt immense guilt. She had not awakened to assist the assaulted girl despite her attempt get Mary's attention by scratching at the door, and beyond that, Mary had failed to protect the girl from ever experiencing that brutal attack in the first place. Apparently, Mary was so distraught over the entire experience that she soon began suffering from insomnia herself. Other girls in the dorm regularly observed Mary pacing the halls all night long. Mary was experiencing horrible nightmares and ultimately delved into such a deep depression that she had to be hospitalized. She never recovered. Instead, Mary sank into such a deep abyss of despair that she could no longer stand it and killed herself.

Unfortunately, death has not alleviated Mary of her guilt over the murder of one of her residents...as she has chosen to return to Pemberton Hall where she now watches over its current residents. Her friendly spirit is always around looking after everyone. Girls who fall asleep without locking their dorm room doors wake up in the morning to find someone's locked the door for them during the night. Mary is also known to turn off lights, televisions, radios, and curling irons that have been left on. It seems her protective nature carries on as she watches over the girls of Pemberton Hall.

Illinois College, Jacksonville

Forty miles west of Springfield sits Illinois College in Jacksonville. Founded in 1829, the college has seen several famous names over the years. Author and abolitionist Harriet Beecher Stowe visited on several occasions while her brother Edward Beecher was president of the college. Other notable guests have included Ralph Waldo Emerson, Samuel Langhorne Clements, otherwise known as Mark Twain, and even Abraham Lincoln. The campus was active in the fight against slavery and assisted with Underground Railroad efforts. Various tunnels still run below the campus from many of its oldest buildings. The college's rich history has been further enhanced by stories of hauntings over the years. Some of the most haunted places on campus include: *Beecher Hall*, the *David A. Smith House*, *Ellis Hall*, *Whipple Hall*, *Fayerweather House*, *Sturtevant Hall*, *Crampton Hall*, the *McGaw Building*, and the *Rammelkamp Chapel*.

The ghost that haunts the *Ellis Hall* women's dorm is said to be that of a distressed girl who failed to get into the sorority she was hoping to pledge and subsequently committed suicide by hanging herself in the closet of her dorm room. Anyone who's lived in that room since has reported unexplained activity...like appliances being turned on or the television suddenly turning off. The door is often discovered to be unlocked whenever anyone returns home after having locked it on his or her way out, and personal items sometimes go missing only to be found in a completely different location several days later. It seems the girl who killed herself couldn't bear to let go and lives on in her old dorm room.

A former female student is also said to haunt another women's dorm, the *Fayerweather House*. Those familiar with the ghost call her "Susie" and she is believed to have also committed suicide in her dorm room, although the reason why is unclear. Paranormal activity includes footsteps, scratching sounds, and other strange noises, as well as lights turning on and off on their own and windows and doors opening and closing independently.

☠ *Whipple Hall* was built in 1882 and is home to several Greek organizations on campus and other offices. In the building's more than one hundred years on campus, it must have seen a strange thing or two, as there have been reports of a gray ghost lurking in the shadows near a staircase inside. Some of the terrified witnesses who have encountered this unidentified gray ghost claim that he has no face, which makes it difficult to determine who he might have been or why he haunts the hall, to say the least.

☠ *Sturtevant Hall* also has its own gray ghost. The apparition of a man in a gray Civil War era uniform has been spotted in the building. In addition to this spectral figure, peculiar sounds are often heard throughout the house as well, including independently flushing toilets. Needless to say, most students prefer not to venture inside this spooky building after dark.

☠ *Crampton Hall* is a male dorm that is haunted by the spirit of a former male student who died in his room, either by suicide or murder made to look like suicide. No one is really knows for sure, but there is no doubt his spirit haunts the place.

☠ Inside the *McGaw Performing Arts building* resides a 1940s era ghost who seems to enjoy observing the theatrical performances.

☠ And inside *Rammelkamp Chapel*, classroom doors are sometimes opened by unseen forces—only to be violently slammed shut moments later. The culprit may be a ghostly woman in white who has a habit of vanishing into thin air whenever she is spotted in the building.

☠ The *David A. Smith House*, built in 1854, is another campus building with a few ghosts. The building currently houses several women's Greek organizations, but was originally a private residence. It's believed that the daughter of the original owner, David Smith, haunts her old house. Effie Smith suffered a tragic and avoidable death in the house, which might explain why she's never left. Her father reportedly never liked her boyfriend and would not give his blessing for the two young lovers to marry. It seems Effie and her boyfriend might have considered eloping because he gave her a ring anyway. In her excitement she etched her name into an attic window with the brilliant diamond stone adorning the engagement ring. There must have been an explosive confrontation between Mr. Smith, Effie, and the boyfriend. The outcome was so devastating that Effie chose to take her own life by leaping to her death from an upstairs window. Some accounts of the story suggest that her forbidden lover might also have died on the property by suffocation after being locked in an attic closet with no means of escape. The tragic ending to this tale of star-crossed young love has forever condemned Miss Effie to the house where she lost her life. Evidence of her presence has been noted on numerous occasions. On especially cold days, it was sometimes possible to see Effie's name etched into the glass of an upstairs windowpane despite the original window on which she scratched her name long being replaced. Additionally, her old rocking chair is still stored in the building's attic to this day. It normally sits facing out one of the windows, but if anyone ever moves it, they can bet it'll be right back in its same spot near the window upon their return. Perhaps Effie sits watching out the window hopefully awaiting the return of her beloved.

One of the most interesting hauntings on campus by far is the story of *Beecher Hall*, as told by author and ghost investigator Troy Taylor. Beecher Hall has stood proudly on the Illinois College campus since 1829 and currently functions as a meeting hall for a few fraternities. Nothing too chilling has been reported there, mainly just unexplained footsteps walking about from one room to another. Of course, there is never anyone actually walking around when the footsteps are heard so they are most definitely of an unearthly origin. But who is it that might be lingering in Beecher Hall? It seems Beecher Hall was once used for medical purposes long before it was a meeting place. At the time cadavers had been stored on the upper floor. But were they supposed to be there? Many attribute the first instances of "body snatching" to the medical students of Illinois College who allegedly stole corpses from nearby hospitals, and sometimes cemeteries, stashing them in Beecher Hall to be used for study purposes. The body-snatching persisted until unfathomable repulsive odors began emanating from the house and the overzealous med students were finally stopped. The removal of the cadavers from the house might have eliminated the foul stench, but something else was left behind. Perhaps the stolen corpses didn't appreciate the free room and board in Beecher Hall while they were stashed on the upper floor, because the footsteps of many of them can still be heard pacing about.

The Robert Allerton Mansion, Monticello

There is a gorgeous mansion on Old Timber Road in Monticello about a thirty-minute drive from Champaign-Urbana that was once privately owned but now belongs to the University of Illinois. Referred to as "The Farms," the extensive property was owned by Robert Henry Allerton whose family owned approximately 80,000 acres of farmland throughout Illinois and the surrounding states. Allerton was a generous man who enjoyed sharing his beautiful estate with family and friends. He even donated more than 6,000 pieces of artwork to the Art Institute of Chicago over the course of his lifetime. One of Mr. Allerton's favorite visitors to the grand mansion was his close companion and possible fiancée Ellen Rand. Ellen lived in Chicago and routinely made the trip to Monticello with Robert's step-mother. Despite their romantic relationship, Ellen and Robert never married. She would eventually marry another man, but Robert remained single his entire life. Years after the university had acquired the estate and Robert and Ellen had both long since passed away, rumors of a ghostly lady in white have floated around about the mansion and the grounds; she is often seen walking around the pond in the back of the house. Inside the house, she is heard walking about and has occasionally been seen near her former room. When her apparition is spotted in the room, she is usually observed to be sitting in a chair looking toward the mirror as though primping for an important event. Witnesses who have seen the ghost in person later identified the woman from photos shown to them as Ellen Rand, Allerton's purported fiancée. Perhaps she loved the home and Robert both so much that she always regretted marrying another man and the only way she could get back what she had given up was to return in death, forever walking the grounds of the spectacular mansion that could have been her home.

Afterword

Well, that's it. We've explored many different hauntings throughout the central and southern regions of Illinois from Springfield to Little Egypt. Not only does the great Prairie State have a rich history, but it also has a plethora of hauntings. From haunted college campuses to Civil War spirits, the full gamut of ghosts seems to be covered. How many states can say that?

Before we conclude, here is more information about the many exciting ghost stories and hauntings throughout Central and Southern Illinois, or to take a tour of some of the Prairie State's most haunted places, contact any of the following organizations.

The American Ghost Society

Description: Founded in 1996, the American Ghost Society researches various hauntings throughout Illinois and offers some of the most popular haunted tours in areas like Decatur, Alton, Lebanon, Jacksonville, and Chicago. The organization is open to new membership.

- Troy Taylor: Founder, Author & Researcher
- Len Adams: Vice President, Chief of Operations & Investigation Coordinator, and Lead Guide for Alton Hauntings Tours

Address: American Ghost Society Business Office, 15 Forest Knolls Estates, Decatur, IL 62521
Phone: (217) 422-1002 or 1-888-446-7859
Website: http://www.prairieghosts.com/ags.html
Email: ttaylor@prairieghosts.com

Springfield Ghost Society

Description: The Springfield Ghost Society investigates reports of paranormal activity in Central Illinois; memberships available.
Contact: Debbie Lowery, Founder and Investigator
Address: 200 State St., Rochester, IL 62563
Phone: (217) 414-4678
Website: http://www.springfieldghostsociety.com
Email: djlowery@sbcglobal.net

Springfield Tours

Description: Springfield Tours offers several different tours, including Lincoln's Ghost Walk and Springfield's Haunted Dead Walk.
Contact: Garret Moffett, Owner and Proprietor
Phone: (217) 502-8687
Website: http://www.SpringfieldWalks.com
Email: Garrett@SpringfieldWalks.com

Antoinette's Haunted Alton Tours

Description: Founded in 1992, Antoinette's Haunted Alton Tours are the original haunted Alton tours that allow participants time to investigate the different sites on the tour.

Contact: Antoinette or Alixandria

Address: RBA/AHHT, P.O. Box 10, Alton, IL 62002

Website: http://www.hauntedalton.com

Email: Info@HauntedAlton.com or Reservations@HauntedAlton.com

Crawford County Ghost Hunters

Description: Founded in 2001, Crawford County Ghost Hunters are a paranormal investigation team probing hauntings and paranormal activity in Illinois and Indiana, particularly Crawford County and surrounding counties.

Contact: Jason Snider, Founder and Lead Investigator

Phone: (618) 843-8011

Website: http://www.crawfordcountyghosthunters.com

Email: Jason_Snider@crawfordcountyghosthunters.com or IllinoisHauntings@yahoo.com

Legends and Lore of Illinois

Description: Legends and Lore of Illinois is a monthly paranormal newsletter that features a new haunted Illinois location in every issue.

Contact: Michael Kleen

Website: http://www.blackoakmedia.org/legendsandlore.html

Email: TheFallen2@gmail.com

Haunted & Paranormal Investigations International

Description: Founded in 2004, Haunted and Paranormal Investigations International first started in Northern California and has since expanded across the country. The group conducts paranormal investigations of documented haunted sites and welcomes new members.

Contact: Shannon McCabe, President
Phone: 1-888-709-4HPI
Website: http://www.hpiparanormal.net
Email: ghost@snmproductionsco.com

Bibliography

Alexander, John. *Ghosts: Washington Revisited*. Atglen, Pennsylvania: Schiffer Publishing Ltd., 1998.

Biles, Roger. *Illinois: A History of the Land and Its People*. DeKalb, Illinois: Northern Illinois University Press, 2005.

Christensen, Jo-Anne. *Ghost Stories of Illinois*. Renton, Washington: Lone Pine Publishing, 2000.

Cohen, Daniel. *The Encyclopedia of Ghosts*. New York, New York: Dorset Press, 1989.

Graczyk, Jim and Donna Boonstra. *Field Guide to Illinois Hauntings*. Alton, Illinois: Whitechapel Productions Press, 2002.

Halicki, Diane and Ellen Robson. *Haunted Highway: The Spirits of Route 66*. Phoenix, Arizona: Golden West Publishers, 1999.

Harrelson, Ralph S. *History and Legend of Lakey*. McLeansboro, Illinois: Hamilton County Historical Society, 1973.

Kachuba, John B. *Ghosthunting Illinois*. Cincinnati, Ohio: Emmis Books, 2005.

Kleen, Michael. *Legends and Lore of Illinois*. Cherry Valley, Illinois: Black Oak Press, 2007.

Krupa, John. "Event at Haskell Park Commemorates Namesake of Beloved Playhouse." *The Telegraph*. Alton, Illinois: The Telegraph, July 30, 2005.

Lewis, Chad and Terry Fisk. *Illinois Road Guide to Haunted Locations*. Eau Claire, Wisconsin: Unexplained Research Publishing, LLC, 2007.

Lewis, Lloyd. *Myths after Lincoln*. Gloucester, Massachusetts: Peter Smith Publisher, Inc., 1973.

Luttrell, Liz. "The Halloween Hauntings of Millikin University." Decatur, Illinois: The *Decaturian*, 2005.

Menzies, Gavin. *1421: The Year China Discovered America*. New York, New York: Harper Perennial, 2008.

Neely, Mark E., Jr. *The Abraham Lincoln Encyclopedia*. New York, New York: Da Capo Books, 1982.

Nickell, Joe. *Entities: Angels, Spirits, Demons, and Other Alien Beings*. Amherst, New York: Prometheus Books, 1995.

Nickless, Mark. *Piasa Bird Monster Plucked*. St. Louis, Missouri: *Outdoors Guide Magazine*, Fall 2004.

O'Conner, Mallory McCane. *Lost Cities of the Ancient Southeast*. Gainesville, Florida: The University Press of Florida, 1995.

Ogden, Tom. *The Complete Idiot's Guide to Ghosts and Hauntings*. Royersford, Pennsylvania: Alpha Books, 1999.

Roberts, Paul Dale. *The Six Types of Haunting Activities*. Available online: http://www.TrueGhostTales.com.

Scott, Beth and Michael Norman. *Haunted Heartland*. New York, New York: Dorset Press, 1991.

Taylor, Troy. *Ghosts of Millikin: The History & Hauntings of Millikin University*. Alton, Illinois: Whitechapel Productions, 2001.

Haunted Decatur Revisited: Ghostly Tales from the Haunted Heart of Illinois. Alton, Illinois: Whitechapel Productions, 2000.

Haunted Illinois. Alton, Illinois: Whitechapel Productions Press, 1999.

History & Hauntings of the Riverbend Region. Alton, Illinois: Whitechapel Productions, 1999.

Weird Ghosts and Strange Phenomena of the Prairie State. Mechanicsburg, Pennsylvania: Stackpole Books, 2008.

Thomas, Benjamin P. *Lincoln's New Salem*. Carbondale, Illinois: Southern Illinois University Press, 1987.

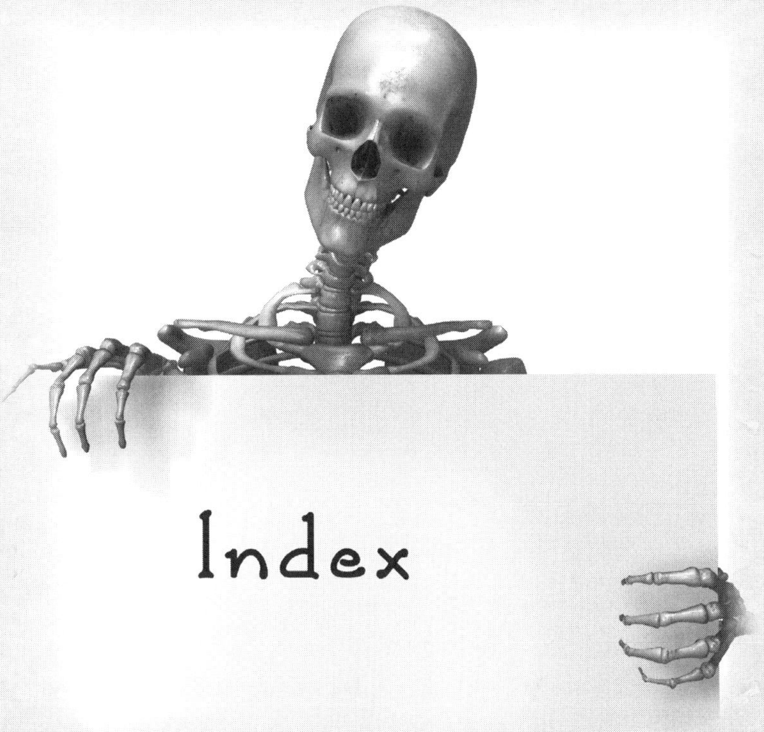

Index